Eleanor Jeans moved to Manchester in 1993 to study the violin at the Roy᷈  that time, she was vice-president of the RNCM Christian Union for a year and ᷈ was a member of the music group, a house group leader and a worship minis᷈

After graduating, she worked for three years as a freelance violinist and᷈ ately 18 schools in Tameside, East Manchester, as well as working with a number of pɪᴏꜰᴇssɪᴏɴᴀ᷈ , the classical Christian ensemble *Wellspring*.

In 2001 Eleanor joined the staff at Holy Trinity Platt as a part-time schools' worker, where she brought together her love of music, her faith and her commitment to children. She has used her music in a number of schools, playing for singing practice, setting up choirs and singing and drama clubs, singing with 3–5s and taking assemblies and RE lessons. Her work has taken her to a wide range of schools, including those with a high ratio of Muslim pupils, as well as to church-aided Catholic schools. It is this diversity that inspired her to develop the play, *This Man Called Jesus*. She worked on the script with two colleagues from Holy Trinity Platt, both professional actors, and drew on her musical experience to write the songs. The play, designed to bridge the gap between church and school, was first performed at Easter in 2003.

In September 2005, Eleanor began work as Director of Music at Emmanuel Church in Loughborough, where she hopes to carry on working with children through music in particular. She continues to freelance as a violinist and teaches both privately and at the University of Leeds.

## IMPORTANT INFORMATION

**Published by**
**The Bible Reading Fellowship**
First Floor, Elsfield Hall
15–17 Elsfield Way, Oxford OX2 8FG
Website: www.brf.org.uk

ISBN 1 84101 434 6
First published 2005
10 9 8 7 6 5 4 3 2 1 0

**Acknowledgments**
Unless otherwise stated, scripture quotations are taken from the Contemporary English Version of the Bible
published by HarperCollins Publishers, copyright © 1991, 1992, 1995 American Bible Society.

**Performance and copyright**
The right to perform *This Man Called Jesus* drama material is included in the purchase price, so long as the
performance is in an amateur context, for instance in church services, schools or holiday club venues. Where
any charge is made to audiences, written permission must be obtained from the author, who can be contacted
through the publishers. A fee or royalties may be payable for the right to perform the script in that context.

A catalogue record for this book is available from the British Library

Printed in Singapore by Craft Print International Ltd

# This Man Called Jesus

An easy-to-run Easter play complete with music and cross-curricular project work

## Eleanor Jeans

*Dedicated to the children and teachers at St Edward's School,*
*Wilbraham School and Heald Place School—and to my family,*
*who are wonderful.*

## ACKNOWLEDGMENTS

First and foremost, thanks to Stephen Mackel and Zoe Longley, who co-wrote the play and worked on the drama side of things; secondly, to all those who came and helped with the original project: Richard Jones (who named the play), Caroline Vere, Geth Griffith, Helen Gray, Ian Gray, Jane Seddon and Chris De La Hoyde. Thanks also to the staff and pupils of St Edward's School (particularly the original performers and their teacher, Louise Parr) for your support and willingness to perform the play.

Thanks must also go to the staff and congregation at Holy Trinity Platt, Manchester, for their encouragement and prayers.

# Contents

# Foreword

Religious Education is a complicated area of the curriculum as it extends far beyond the school institution and into the outside life of the pupil. Dealing with the spiritual, and structuring it in a way that children can make sense of, is a difficult and challenging area for most classroom teachers. There is a need to make more cross-curricular links in order to present the RE syllabus in a way that is not just accessible but interesting enough for the children to empathize with the subject matter and understand the complicated themes within the narrative. Too often, teachers assume that children understand the themes and issues, but, in my experience as a practitioner, if we scratch a little further below the surface the children reveal little understanding beyond the literal.

When I was approached by Eleanor Jeans to pilot her script—then in its draft form—using *my* class, I was delighted. As a drama specialist, I am well aware of the lack of drama in an already over-packed curriculum. *This Man Called Jesus* has been created in such a way that the chunks are bite-sized and can be taught in isolation or as a whole (which is how my class approached it). The children seized on the familiar narrative, but delighted in the empowerment of modifying and taking ownership of the story by referencing previous learning and making sense through drama, using a variety of conventions such as role-play, writing in role, improvization and devising from a given stimulus or starting point in the Easter story.

We worked through the complicated and quite adult themes of betrayal, sacrifice, reflection, guilt, anticipation, duty and commitment. The powerful use of music in this piece not only complemented the script, but also extended the understanding of the story over and beyond the spoken word. It was absorbed into the children's subliminal understanding as they sang the songs with passion and showed committed performances as citizens of Jerusalem or as Jesus' disciples voicing their grief at his death.

From my point of view, it was an exciting and challenging product which delivered all that it promised and had echoes of the Lloyd Webber musical *Jesus Christ Superstar*—but for children! It was a pleasure to work alongside Eleanor Jeans. She enthused me with her inspirational and spiritual qualities and it was a privilege to be involved in such a beautifully crafted piece of work.

*Louise Atkinson, Primary teacher, Blue Zone 1 After School Study Centre, Moss Side, Manchester*

# Introduction

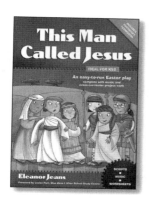

'There aren't many songs about the resurrection, are there?' said a colleague of mine one Easter. 'Why don't you do something about it?'

This was just one of the comments that motivated me to set the ball rolling with *This Man Called Jesus*. It was a while before things started moving, but I began to realize how little we really celebrate the amazing festival of Easter. It was through Jesus' death and resurrection 2000 years ago that the Christian Church was born, but I have become increasingly aware of the fact that, for many people, the word 'Easter' is associated with bunnies and Easter eggs rather than Jesus. I'm not saying that there is anything wrong with bunnies and Easter eggs—after all, they do symbolize new life, which is what Jesus gave when he died on the cross and rose again—but my main motivation for writing *This Man Called Jesus* is to help children to understand the true meaning of Easter.

In January 2003, Stephen Mackel, Zoe Longley (two actors who help me with assemblies in local schools) and I began to think of ways we could help children hear the Easter story. We were well aware of how much children learn when they are actually taking part in something and so began to write the Easter story as a play for Key Stage 2 children to perform.

What transpired was a five-act play with six songs, beginning with Jesus' triumphant entry into Jerusalem and ending with his death and resurrection, using words that adhere closely to the original Bible texts. We also linked the play to other parts of the National Curriculum to give the play *This Man Called Jesus* the potential of being project-based.

The whole production was tried and tested at St Edward's School, Rusholme in Manchester, where we worked with a Year 4 class and their excellent teacher, Louise Parr, who helped us fine-tune the script. The children performed the play at Easter after a rehearsal time of around half a term, with one or two rehearsals each week. Since then, part of the play has been performed again and we have worked with other local schools on individual sections of the play.

## HOW TO USE THIS BOOK

This book is divided into four distinct sections.

**Section One** contains all the information you will need to prepare for the production itself, such as the scene synopsis, characters, props, costumes, stage set-up and rehearsal schedules.

**Section Two** contains links to other curriculum subjects, with lesson plans, drama workshops, vocal warm-up ideas and ideas for art, design and ICT. Feel free to use as much or as little of the curriculum links as you like. If need be, the play can stand on its own without any of the links being used.

**Section Three** contains ideas and information to help you link the material to your RE syllabus.

**Section Four** contains the full script of the play. The five scenes can be approached as a single performance, or divided up and performed by different classes on the same day or over a week. It is also possible to take just one scene (such as Scene 2, 'The last meal together', which one school did this year) and perform it in isolation. The script of the play closely follows the Bible text, using the wording of the Contemporary English Version.

Finally, there are two sections where you will find a photocopiable worksheet for each song, so that you can give copies to each performer, or even include the audience if you would like some interactive input, as well as the sheet music for the songs.

Much of the material in this book is based on the work of the children who piloted the project. We hope you enjoy preparing and performing the play as much as we did.

## THIS MAN CALLED JESUS CD

A CD of the music for the play can be obtained direct from the author. For more information, e-mail contact@thisman.co.uk or visit the website www.thisman.co.uk.

## SECTION ONE

# Preparation

# Scene synopsis

In order to gain a clear overview of the play as a whole, it is advisable to read through the full scene synopsis before starting work. We would also advise taking time to read the Bible passages given for each scene, so that you have a firm idea of the original storyline. Using a modern translation such as the Good News Bible or the Contemporary English Version is helpful.

### SCENE 1

Bible references: Matthew 21:1–17; 22:15–22 and 26:1–16

## Jesus enters Jerusalem

Jesus enters Jerusalem with his disciples for the final time, to a loud welcome and shouts of 'Hallelujah'. He gets angry when he sees how the people are treating the temple—turning it into a market square. Some of the chief priests and religious leaders become very jealous of Jesus and begin to plot how they can get rid of him. One of Jesus' disciples, Judas, is asked to betray Jesus.

**Songs**
Jesus is coming
We want rid of him

### SCENE 2

Bible references: Luke 22:7–34

## The last meal together

Jesus and his disciples meet in an upstairs room of a local house to eat together and celebrate the Passover festival. Jesus tells his friends that he is soon to die. He also warns them that one of them is going to betray him.

### SCENE 3

Bible references: Matthew 26:36–68 and 27:11–26

## The garden of Gethsemane

Jesus and the disciples go to the garden of Gethsemane to pray. But while they are there, Judas arrives with armed guards to hand Jesus over to the authorities.

Jesus is then put on trial. He is found innocent but, even so, is sentenced to death, taking the place of a murderer named Barabbas.

**Song**
Why do we call it Good Friday?

### SCENE 4

Bible references: Matthew 27:27–44

## The crucifixion

Barabbas sits in his cell, waiting to be released, as Jesus is led to the hill to be crucified in his place.

**Song**
Barabbas' song

### SCENE 5

Bible references: Luke 24:1–12, 36–53; John 20:1–29 and 21:15–25

## The resurrection

The disciples sit together, mourning the death of their friend and leader, Jesus. Mary and Salome arrive back with some amazing news. Jesus' body is not in the tomb! Jesus proves that he has come alive again by visiting the disciples. His appearances convince them that what Jesus had said about himself is true. He is indeed the Son of God and the mystery of the resurrection is proof of his authenticity.

**Songs**
Clap your hands, shout hallelujah
Jesus is living

# Casting the play

If you have a large class, or are working with more than one class, so that there are too many children to give them each a part in the play, the class can be split into three separate areas of involvement, all of which are equally important.

1 Actors
2 Singers and musicians
3 Production team

## ACTORS

Here is a list of things you could consider when choosing actors for the play.

Some parts are written particularly for those who are gifted at acting but don't feel able or don't want to say too many lines; others are written for those gifted at reading out loud, but for whom acting is more of a challenge. Some parts have a large quantity of lines to learn; others simply have one or two.

Information is given below about each character, and suggestions are offered as to what skills are needed for each part. If you have more children than parts, everyone can be given a role by adding to the number of friends and enemies of Jesus. If you have fewer children than parts, the roles can be doubled up. For example, the girl with the perfume could also play the part of one of the servant girls.

### Narrators 1, 2, 3, 4 and 5
❖ Appear in Scenes 1–5
❖ Large speaking roles
❖ Good readers to stand on/off-stage and speak into microphones
❖ Acting ability required
❖ Good reading skills required

### Jesus
❖ Appears in Scenes 1, 2, 3 and 5
❖ A carpenter by trade; the Son of God by birth
❖ Good acting skills required

### Peter, James and John
❖ Appear in Scenes 1, 2, 3 and 5
❖ Jesus' closest friends; fishermen by profession
❖ Good acting skills required
❖ James has the least to say and Peter has the most

### Judas Iscariot
❖ Appears in Scenes 1, 2, 3 and 5
❖ Jesus' friend, but then betrayed him
❖ Reasonable acting skills required
❖ Has only a couple of lines to say

### Andrew
❖ Appears in Scenes 1, 2, 3 and 5
❖ Jesus' friend
❖ Reasonable acting skills required
❖ Has only a couple of lines to say

### Thomas
❖ Appears in Scenes 1, 2, 3 and 5
❖ Jesus' friend
❖ Reasonable acting skills required
❖ Has only a couple of lines to say

### Other disciples
❖ Appear in Scenes 1, 2, 3 and 5
❖ Jesus' closest friends
❖ Good acting skills required
❖ Up to six characters, making twelve altogether with Peter, James, John, Andrew, Thomas and Judas Iscariot
❖ Non-speaking parts

### Mary and Salome
❖ Appear in Scenes 1, 2, 3 and 5
❖ Followers of Jesus
❖ Reasonable acting skills required
❖ Have a few lines, mainly in Scene 5

### Crowd (three to five people)

- ❖ Appear in Scene 1
- ❖ Welcome Jesus into Jerusalem
- ❖ Less acting skill required, but need to be enthusiastic

### Chief priests 1, 2 and 3

- ❖ Appear in Scene 1
- ❖ Try to trick and catch Jesus out
- ❖ Less acting skill required, but need to be enthusiastic
- ❖ These parts have only a couple of lines

### Accusers 1, 2 and 3

- ❖ Appear in Scenes 1 and 3
- ❖ Paid by the authorities to tell lies against Jesus in court
- ❖ Less acting skill required, but need to be enthusiastic
- ❖ Have a number of lines in Scene 3

### Caiaphas, the high priest

- ❖ Appears in Scene 3
- ❖ Small acting role with a couple of lines
- ❖ Needs to be a clear and strong speaker

### Girl with a bottle of perfume

- ❖ Appears in Scene 1
- ❖ Pours perfume on to Jesus' head
- ❖ Reasonable acting skills required
- ❖ Non-speaking part

### Servant girls 1, 2 and 3

- ❖ Appear in Scene 3
- ❖ In the temple courtyard during Jesus' trial
- ❖ Recognize Peter
- ❖ Less acting skill required, but need to be enthusiastic
- ❖ Small speaking parts

### Pilate, the Roman governor

- ❖ Appears in Scene 3
- ❖ Gives the people a chance to free Jesus
- ❖ Small acting role with a couple of lines
- ❖ Needs to be a clear and strong speaker

### Malchus, the temple guard

- ❖ Appears in Scene 3
- ❖ Has his ear chopped off by Peter and is then healed by Jesus.
- ❖ No speaking lines, but needs to be a relatively good actor

### Barabbas

- ❖ Appears in Scene 4
- ❖ Convicted criminal
- ❖ Crowds choose to release him instead of Jesus
- ❖ Good acting skills required
- ❖ Has no speaking lines, but is the only character on stage in Scene 4

## SINGERS AND MUSICIANS

The part of Barabbas requires a good singing voice. If, however, the child playing Barabbas isn't a good singer, another child may be chosen to sing the solo part while the actor is on stage. If you are working with a large group of children, you might also have enough people to form a small orchestra. If this is the case, begin to identify which instruments the children play and to what standard. If you are working with a small group, the songs can be performed with the backing of a single instrument such as a piano.

## PRODUCTION TEAM

You will need a group of children to produce items such as posters, programmes and tickets for the performance, to draw together the props, create costumes and produce visual displays. If you do not have enough children to provide a separate production team, these tasks could be covered by staff or helpers, or done as a whole class outside of rehearsal time.

Here is a list of some of the things that the production group could do. This list isn't exhaustive and some other ideas are mentioned in Section Two as part of the cross-curriculum links.

### Advertising

- ❖ Taking photographs of the rehearsal process
- ❖ Drawing or painting characters or scenes
- ❖ Designing and making posters
- ❖ Designing and making programmes (you may wish to include features such as wordsearches, puzzles, news articles, stories, profiles of the cast, and so on)
- ❖ Designing and making tickets for the show

## Props and costumes

❖ Making palm branches to wave at the beginning and end of the show
❖ Making a crown of thorns
❖ Making a cross
❖ Making headdresses for Mary and Salome
❖ Designing T-shirts or costumes for the whole cast and production crew

## Research

❖ Looking at the history of Jerusalem
❖ Researching and recreating a Passover feast
❖ Looking at the Bible stories that influence the script
❖ Finding out the relevance of palm branches and donkeys
❖ Researching the different characters in the play

## Technical

❖ Creating sound effects or special lighting as required
❖ Making a video, slide show or static display to represent the crucifixion, to be shown during Scene 4

## On the night

❖ Providing a compère to make any necessary announcements
❖ Providing 'front of house' to show the audience to their seats
❖ Providing a prompt, with a copy of the whole script—in case any of the actors forget their lines
❖ Providing sound or lighting operators

# Props and costumes

*This Man Called Jesus* is designed to use the minimum number of costumes and props. Those deemed to be essential to the play are outlined below, but do feel free to use others as you feel appropriate. When we performed the play, all the children wore T-shirts, which we designed and the children subsequently kept as souvenirs. You could ask those children who are narrators, enemies or friends of Jesus to wear different coloured T-shirts depending on their role. At the point where he betrays Jesus, Judas could change the colour T-shirt he wears. Headdresses could be used to distinguish between the main characters.

Further suggestions about props and costumes can be found in the chapter on Design and Technology on page 27 and within the play itself.

## SCENE 1

### JESUS ENTERS JERUSALEM

 **Props**

- ❖ Palm branches
- ❖ Coats
- ❖ Perfume jar
- ❖ CD or cassette player (optional)
- ❖ Projector and screen (optional)

## SCENE 2

### THE LAST MEAL TOGETHER

 **Props**

- ❖ Dishes
- ❖ Bread (naan, pitta or unleavened bread made in technology)
- ❖ Cups
- ❖ Rug
- ❖ Music to play as the children eat

## SCENE 3

### THE GARDEN OF GETHSEMANE

 **Props**

- ❖ Peter's sword
- ❖ Crown of thorns
- ❖ A throne for Caiaphas and Pilate
- ❖ Large plants for the garden of Gethsemane

 **Costumes**

- ❖ Soldiers' outfits

## SCENE 4

### THE CRUCIFIXION

 **Props**

- ❖ Montage of crosses
- ❖ Project work on Barabbas
- ❖ Optional atmospheric lighting with jail gobo (filter for stage lights)

## SCENE 5

### THE RESURRECTION

 **Props**

- ❖ Rug
- ❖ Folded grave clothes
- ❖ Dishes
- ❖ Cups
- ❖ Palm branches

# Stage set-up

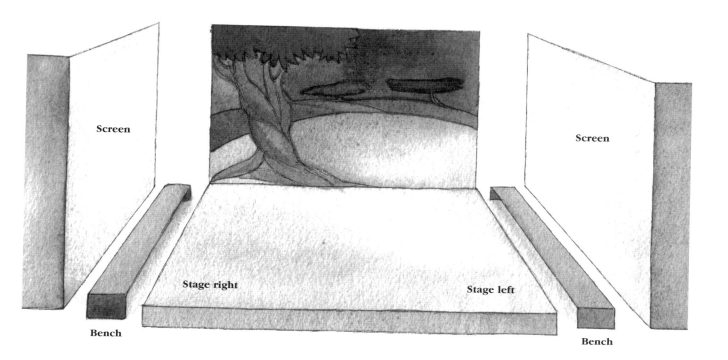

The stage needs to be divided into three areas as follows.

## STAGE LEFT

This is where the action involving Jesus and the disciples takes place. Stage left is the *right*-hand side of the stage for the audience, and the *left*-hand side for the actors standing on stage and looking out into the audience.

## STAGE RIGHT

This is where the action involving the enemies of Jesus and his betrayal takes place. Stage right is the *left*-hand side of the stage for the audience, and the *right*-hand side for the actors standing on stage and looking out into the audience.

## CENTRE STAGE

This is where action involving both the disciples and enemies of Jesus takes place, and where Barabbas sits during Scene 4.

You may find it helpful to have a long bench on either side of the stage, where the cast can sit when they are not on stage.

You will need to place a projector screen at the centre back of the stage if a slide show or video is to be shown during Scene 4. If you are using a cross, this also needs to be placed centre back stage. A crown of thorns can then be placed on the cross during Scene 4.

It will be helpful to have a screened-off area on either side of the stage to store props and costumes until they are needed. The prompt can also use this area.

It would also be helpful to have microphones available for the narrators, and an area to one side, front of stage, where they can sit during the performance. They can then either remain seated or stand to read their parts, depending on visibility and acoustics.

# Rehearsal schedule

*This Man Called Jesus* is designed to go from page to stage in approximately six weeks, with a minimum of two hours per week allocated to rehearsal and project work. Further time, preferably outside of school hours, will need to be set aside as private study for those children with lines to learn.

Below is a sample rehearsal schedule suggesting how the play can be prepared and rehearsed in this timeframe. With larger classes, the children can be split into three groups. With smaller classes, all the children may be involved in all aspects of the play, so more time may be needed to ensure that everything is ready.

As mentioned in the Introduction on page 7, *This Man Called Jesus* can be approached with a high degree of flexibility. Please don't feel that you have to do everything that is suggested: each performance of the play will be different. You may only have time to prepare one or two scenes, without props or costumes. You may wish to rehearse the full play, but not follow any of the project work suggestions. Whatever you decide, the main aim is that you enjoy putting on the show. The suggested timeframe and activities are offered as a guide to help you to achieve this aim, so please don't feel tied down by any suggestions that don't fit with your individual needs.

## WEEK ONE

### All together

Photocopy the script on pages 50–59 so that everyone has their own copy. Read through the script as a class. Talk about the different roles involved in putting on a play from 'page to stage'—actors, musicians and production—all of which are equally important. Tell the children that by the next time you meet they must have decided which section they would rather work in, and which would be their second choice.

As a whole group, devise a set of rules, or a contract, that you will all stick to while working on the play. Suggestions for this might include:

❖ To encourage teamwork
❖ To support each other
❖ To try new things
❖ To put in 100 per cent effort

Lead the whole class in a drama workshop, warming up physically and vocally before you start. Be aware, during the improvization exercises, of those who may have the ability to take on main roles, such as Jesus. Try to let go of presumptions: some children may surprise you by being unexpectedly creative.

Photocopy the songs so that everyone has his or her own copy. Start to familiarize yourself with the words and music for the songs. The song sheets and notation can be found on pages 62–78. A CD of the songs (with backing tracks and full performance of the songs) is also available direct from the author via the website www.thisman.co.uk.

## WEEK TWO

### Actors

Get the children to read set parts of the script to audition for different parts. Use some of the improvization exercises on pages 23–24 to ensure that they can perform as well as read and speak well.

When you have made your decision, split the actors into three groups as follows:

Group One: Jesus and the narrators
Group Two: Jesus' friends
Group Three: Jesus' enemies

In these groups, get the children to work through their lines, going over any unknown phrases or words with each other. Encourage the children to take home copies of their script and look at Scenes 1 and 2 for next week.

### Singers and musicians

Audition the children for the solo parts by getting them to sing a song they know well. If you have enough children in the group to form a small orchestra, identify which instruments the children play and to what standard. Allocate certain instruments to certain songs, according to what you have available. For example, you could allocate recorders to the song 'Why do we call it Good Friday?' and chime bars and glockenspiels to the song 'Clap your hands, shout hallelujah'.

## All together

As a group, learn the songs 'Jesus is coming' and 'Jesus is living'. Give the chosen soloist 'Barabbas' song' to look at and to start to learn at home, or in singing lessons if they are available in school time.

## Production

Look through the script and identify the different props and costumes needed throughout the show. Allocate them to different groups of children. Start to work on designing the T-shirts or costumes for the cast and production team. At the end of the session, have a group vote to decide which designs to choose. Designs not chosen can make part of the display in the entrance hall on the day of the performance. Think of ideas to include on posters.

### WEEK THREE

## Actors

Rehearse Scenes 1 and 2. As already mentioned in 'stage set-up', you may find it helpful, when rehearsing and performing, to have all of the action involving Jesus and his friends taking place on one side of the stage, and all of the action involving Jesus' enemies or his betrayal on the other side. This will help the children to know where on stage they should be, and

will also help the audience to follow what is happening and who is who. If all the cast are involved, use the centre of the stage.

Encourage the actors always to look forward when speaking and to speak slower than they would normally. Remind them that if there are a large number of people moving around on stage, things can get confusing, so they need to try to keep unnecessary movement to a minimum. You will always have some children not directly involved when rehearsing. Encourage these children to watch what is happening on stage and take notes (so that, when you come back to it later, they can all help each other out), or to look at their own lines and practise them. Remember that children not only need to know their own part of the play, but also the sections on either side.

## Singers and musicians

Recap the songs 'Jesus is coming' and 'Jesus is living'. Start to consider the use of instruments as well as voices. Go through the vocals of the songs 'We want rid of him' and 'Barabbas' song' in front of the group, so that the soloists can begin to get used to performing in front of people.

## Production

Take photographs of the actors and musicians rehearsing, to put in the programme.

Make a video, create a slide show or produce a static display depicting the crucifixion. This can be shown while 'Barabbas' song' is being performed. Research the Internet or books to find suitable images. Check with copyright holders if you are unsure whether or not you need permission to use their material.

### WEEK FOUR

## Actors

Run through Scenes 1 and 2 without scripts. Rehearse Scenes 3 and 5. Remember to continue each scene from where the previous one ended. You will find it helpful to write notes recording the movements the children make on stage, which can be used in later rehearsals to save time.

## Singers and musicians

Recap the songs 'Jesus is coming', 'Jesus is living', 'We want rid of him' and 'Barabbas' song'. Add instruments into 'We want rid of him'. Learn 'Why do we call it Good Friday?'

## Production

Design and make bright posters. Include the name and time of the show, the location and ticket price and so on. Put the posters up around the school and local area to advertise the show.

Make a crown of thorns and palm branches.

## Actors

Rehearse Scene 4 with the video, slide show or display that the production team have come up with. Rehearse Scenes 3 and 5 without scripts. Try to run the whole play, leaving appropriate spaces for the songs.

## Singers and musicians

Recap the four songs learnt so far. Add instruments into the song 'Why do we call it good Friday?' Learn the song 'Clap your hands, shout hallelujah'.

## Production

Design and start to make the programme. Make it interesting and fun by including wordsearches, puzzles and articles, as well as the cast list and a summary of the plot.

Make the T-shirts or costumes. Include headdresses for Mary and Salome if required.

## Actors

Run twice through the whole play without scripts (or songs).

## Singers and musicians

Add instruments into the song 'Clap your hands, shout hallelujah'.

Run through all the songs twice.

## Production

Design, make and sell tickets. Finish off any props, costumes or programmes that need finalizing.

## All together

Time for the dress rehearsal! Run through the whole thing with props, costumes, songs, prompt and compère. If you have a separate production team, invite them to act as the audience. After you have completed the dress rehearsal, get feedback from the actors, musicians and production team on all aspects of the show.

Make any little changes needed so that you can be confident that everything is ready for the performance itself.

Throughout, don't forget the most important thing: make sure you are all enjoying it!

# Rehearsal diary

So that you and the children have a record of the whole process of the play from page to stage, it is recommended that everyone keeps a rehearsal diary. This helps you to reflect on what has happened and to look forward to what will happen next. It records what the children, as individuals, are thinking and feeling, as well as what they have learnt and enjoyed, and is a good place for them to outline any struggles they may be having.

Below is an example of a rehearsal diary, which should be filled in after every session.

## This Man Called Jesus

Name: _____ Date: _____

Role: _____

Today we… _____

What I enjoyed most today was… _____

What I enjoyed least today was… _____

Two things I learnt today about acting and putting on a play are…

_____

_____

Two things I learnt today about the story of Jesus are…

_____

_____

Before next time I need to:

Practise… _____

Work on… _____

Learn… _____

Next time I would really like to try… _____

Next time I need to… _____

Reproduced with permission from *This Man Called Jesus* published by BRF 2005 (1 84101 434 6) www.barnabasinschools.org.uk

**SECTION TWO**

# Curriculum links

# Drama

### ENGLISH 1: SPEAKING AND LISTENING
(Key Stage 2)

#### Unit 4: Drama

To participate in a wide range of drama activities and to evaluate their own and others' contributions, pupils should be taught to:

a) create, adapt and sustain different roles, individually and in groups.
b) use character, action and narrative to convey story, themes, emotions and ideas in plays they devise and script.
c) use dramatic techniques to explore characters and issues (for example, hot seating, flashback).
d) evaluate how they and others have contributed to the overall effectiveness of performances.

#### Unit 11: Drama activities

The range should include:

a) improvization and working in role.
b) scripting and performing in plays.
c) responding to performances.

## Introduction

There are many different drama games and exercises that can and should be used to warm up the children before rehearsal, or as part of the audition process to see how creative and expressive they can be.

There may be games and exercises that prove especially popular with your class: don't be afraid to go back and use them again. Repetition can be very effective. Below are some games and exercises that you may find useful. If you find yourself running out of games, you may wish to visit the *This Man Called Jesus* weblink www.thisman.co.uk for alternative ideas.

## Vocal exercises

Practise some tongue twisters such as the suggestions given below. You may have other favourites to add to the mix.

*A tutor who tooted the flute*
*Tried to tutor two tooters to toot.*
*Said the two to the tutor,*
*'Is it harder to toot, or to tutor two tooters to toot?'*

*Red lorry, yellow lorry, red lorry, yellow lorry.*

*If Peter Piper picked a peck of pickled peppers,*
*Where's the peck of pickled peppers Peter Piper picked?*

*She sells seashells by the seashore.*

*How much wood would a woodchuck chuck*
*If a woodchuck could chuck wood?*

*You've no need to light a night-light*
*On a light night like tonight,*
*For a night-light's light's a slight light,*
*And tonight's a night that's light.*

*Three free throws.*

*Please pay promptly.*

*Fat frogs flying past fast.*

*The boot black bought the black boot back.*

*Flash message!*

## Focal exercises

### Mirror images

In pairs, get one person to lead and the other to mirror exactly what their partner does. Get someone else from the group to watch to see if they can work out who is leading and who is following. This is a controlled exercise. The aim is that an observer shouldn't be able to tell who is leading and who is following.

### Follow my leader

Get the whole class to follow and exactly copy one of the pupils in everything that they do. Every now and then, get them to freeze, to see if you can catch out members of the group who are not copying exactly.

### Keys

One child stands with their back to the rest of the class and with a set of keys at their feet. Starting at the opposite end of the room, the rest of the class have to creep up silently and try to retrieve the keys and get them back to the other end. Every three or more seconds, the first child can turn around, at which point the rest of the class freezes. Anyone caught moving is sent back to the beginning.

This can be played as an individual or a team game: either the first child to get the keys back wins, or the whole class work together, passing the keys from one to another to get them back. If the person with the keys is caught, the keys go back to their original position.

## Physical exercises

### Protect me from my enemy!

Split the class into groups of three. One child in each group chooses one of the others as a protector and the other as an enemy. They have to move around the room, trying at all times to keep their protector in between themselves and their enemy. Freeze every now and then to see how they are doing, and to get them to change roles.

### Port and starboard

Identify the four walls as Port, Starboard, Bow and Stern. The children walk around the room and, as you call out the four areas, they have to be the first to get to that wall without running or knocking anyone over. You can gradually add in other commands, such as 'climb the rigging', where the children mime climbing a ladder; 'scrub the decks', where they fall on to their knees and scrub the floor; 'captain's coming', where they stand to attention and say 'Yes Sir'; 'submarines', where they lie on their back with an arm or leg in the air; and so on. The last person to complete each command is out of the game and the game continues until just one person is left.

### Go if…

All the children except one sit on chairs in a circle. The one without a chair stands in the centre and says 'Go if…' followed by a statement that is true about themselves, such as 'Go if you are wearing green socks' or 'Go if you have held hands with somebody in this room' or 'Go if you have ever been told off by the head teacher'. Everyone to whom the command applies must get off his or her seat and swap with someone else who has also got up. The aim is for the person in the centre to get to an empty seat, leaving somebody else to do the next 'Go if…'.

## Improvization exercises

### What are you doing?

All stand in a circle. The first person mimes any action they want. The next asks them, 'What are you doing?' The first replies with an answer that is completely different from what they are actually doing, and the second person then has to mime what the first has just said. The third asks the second, 'What are you doing?' to which they reply something completely different, which the third person then has to mime, and so on. This continues until everyone in the circle has had at least one go.

### Story consequences

In small groups, give the whole class two key words. They have to write the opening of a story including the key words. They then pass their story round to the next group. Give the class two more key words. Each group has to continue the story now in front of them with the two new words. Do this once more to end the story, then pass them round one more time. In their groups, the children then have to act out the story in front of them for the rest of the group.

## Slide shows

In groups or as a whole class, give the children a topic or scenario, such as a trip to the cinema, a family meal, a football match or a rollercoaster ride. The children then have 30 seconds to make a still image that represents this scenario. A good way to get the children to freeze is to pretend to hold a camera, count down '3, 2, 1, click', and take an imaginary photograph of them, in a pose which they then have to hold.

This exercise can be developed by sending one or two children out of the room while the 'slide' is being prepared, then bringing them back and asking them to guess what it is depicting. Also, you can bring the 'slides' to life by getting the children to add five seconds of sound to the picture before freezing again.

## What do you mean?

Put all the children in pairs. They have to choose an emotion from a list—such as happy, sad, angry, lonely, hurt—and say to their partner, 'What do you mean?' in that emotion. Their partner has to guess which emotion they are expressing.

This can be done using only the voice, only facial or bodily expressions, or by combining all three.

# English

## ENGLISH 2: READING
(Key Stage 2)

### Unit 2: Understanding texts
Pupils should be taught to:

a) use inference and deduction.
b) look for meaning beyond the literal.
c) make connections between different parts of a text (for example, how stories begin and end, what has been included and omitted in information writing).
d) use their knowledge of other texts they have read.

### Unit 3
Pupils should be taught to:

c) obtain specific information through detailed reading.

### Unit 6
To read texts with greater accuracy and understanding, pupils should be taught to identify and comment on features of English at word, sentence and text level, using appropriate terminology.

## Comparison exercises
Have available a selection of different versions of the Bible, such as:

❖ New Century Version: International Children's Bible
❖ The Lion Storyteller Bible
❖ *THE MESSAGE*
❖ Good News Bible
❖ Contemporary English Version
❖ Contemporary English Version Popular Schools Bible
❖ Contemporary English Version Youth Bible
❖ New International Version

Alternatively, use a local dialect translation, such as *The Bible in Cockney* by Mike Coles, published by BRF. Select one or more Bible passages listed in the 'Scene synopsis' chapter on page 10. In groups, compare the different versions at word, sentence and text level. Make a list of the differences and similarities. Finally, in groups or individually, write your own version of the text, based on your understanding of the different versions you have looked at.

## Comprehension exercises
Select one or more Bible passages listed in the 'Scene synopsis' chapter on page 10. Identify any words that the children don't understand. Have dictionaries available for the children to look up the words and discuss the meanings together.

## Information exercises
Using an atlas of the Bible, discuss together the geographical location of the biblical story. Using a modern atlas, locate the area where the story took place and compare it with the Bible atlas, identifying the geographical changes between the Bible atlas and the modern-day atlas. Write a report on your findings.

## CURRICULUM LINK

**ENGLISH 3: WRITING**

(Key Stage 2)

### Unit 9: Breadth of study

The range of purposes for writing should include:

a) to imagine and explore feelings and ideas, focusing on creative uses of language and how to interest the reader.

b) to inform and explain, focusing on the subject matter and how to convey it in sufficient detail for the reader.

c) to persuade, focusing on how arguments and evidence are built up and language used to convince the reader.

d) to review and comment on what has been read, seen or heard, focusing on both the topic and the writer's view of it.

### Unit 10

Pupils should also be taught to use writing to help their thinking, investigating, organizing and learning.

## Barabbas

Creative writing exercises are used as a means to explore the character of Barabbas in greater detail, with the children being encouraged to write from his point of view. The finished work could be combined into a single monologue, or one particular piece could be chosen for the performance itself, with the others being included in the programme. Ideas for creative writing can be found in Section Three: RE links, pages 38–47.

## A day in the life of...

As a class, create a magazine or newspaper for other pupils, staff or visitors to read. Decide on a title for your publication and get the children to contribute articles written from the point of view of different characters in the play. Allow them to choose to report on a single day in that character's life, or reflect on the range of events that took place over the whole period of the play. You could link the exercise to art, by creating a cartoon for the newspaper; and a link to ICT might be to take photos of characters and add them in. Collect a few newspapers and programmes together for the children to study and see what sort of things are included in them.

## Puzzles

In groups or individually, create wordsearches using words that link in to the storyline of the play. Alternatively, create a crossword about one of the characters, or devise some puzzles based on characters in the play. Choose a selection of the finished work to put into the programme and use the other pieces to create a display.

## Role play

Select one or more Bible passages listed in the 'Scene synopsis' chapter on page 10. Ask the children to rewrite some of the stories in their own words, thinking about different audiences: children, adults, those for whom English is an additional language, or for reading out loud. Think about the most important points in the story and their meaning.

# Design and technology

## CURRICULUM LINK

**DESIGN AND TECHNOLOGY**
(Key Stage 2)

### Unit 2: Working with tools, equipment, materials and components to make quality products

Pupils should be taught to:

a)  select appropriate tools and techniques for making their product.
b)  suggest alternative ways of making their product, if first attempts fail.
c)  explore the sensory qualities of materials and how to use materials and processes.
d)  measure, mark out, cut and shape a range of materials, and assemble, join and combine components and materials accurately.
e)  use finishing techniques to strengthen and improve the appearance of their product, using a range of equipment including ICT.
f)  follow safety procedures for food safety and hygiene.

### Unit 5: Breadth of study

c)  Design and make assignments using a range of materials, including electrical and mechanical components, food, mouldable materials, stiff and flexible sheet materials, and textiles.

### Designing the set for the play

Try to design the set itself. You could use computers to do this and so link in with ICT. Think about the story and each scene in turn, and work out what things you need in each set and what background you might need. This could also link with art and design.

### Designing the costumes

Design and make costumes. In the original perform-ance, we used specially designed T-shirts as simple costumes. If you were to use T-shirts, a design and technology idea would be to design logos and investigate different ways of printing them on to T-shirts, taking into consideration which colours work best together. This could also link into ICT.

If you were to use costumes rather than T-shirts, pupils could investigate textiles and find out about the types of clothes worn in New Testament times.

### Designing the props

Design and make the props for the play, using the props lists on page 14.

### Designing a cross

Make a cross out of wood or papier mâché. Investigate different types of crosses and how the two pieces would be joined together.

### Designing palm branches

You will need palm branches for all of the children except Jesus and the narrators. There are various ways to make them, ranging from rolling up newspaper and cutting down the side until the branches splay out, to using small pieces of thin wood or strong card and designing palm leaves to resemble real palm branches. Children could investigate which of these methods would be more useful, by looking at strength, colour, shape and materials.

## Making unleavened bread

In Scene 3, one of the props is unleavened bread. You can buy this type of bread from a supermarket (Matzo) or use pitta bread. However, recipes for unleavened bread are readily available, so pupils could try making their own. You may wish to try a selection of recipes to find out which one works best. An extension of this activity would be to find out what yeast is and what effect it has when used in breadmaking.

Here is a simple recipe.

**Ingredients**
525g self-raising flour
40g butter
Level teaspoon of salt
Two teaspoons of sugar
425ml mixture of milk and water

**Method**
1. Preheat oven to 200°C.
2. Sift the flour into a bowl with the salt and sugar and rub in the butter. Then add the milk and water to make a sticky dough.
3. Knead the dough until just smooth.
4. Press the dough into a round shape, 1.5cm thick, and place on to a greased baking tray.
5. Bake in the preheated oven for 45 minutes. Cool on a wire rack.

# Art and design

## ART AND DESIGN

(Key Stage 2)

### Unit 1: Exploring and developing ideas

Pupils should be taught to:

a) record from experience and imagination, to select and record from first-hand observation and to explore ideas for different purposes.

b) question and make thoughtful observations about starting points, and select ideas to use in their work.

c) collect visual and other information to help them develop their ideas, including using a sketchbook.

### Unit 2: Investigating and making art, craft and design

Pupils should be taught to:

a) investigate and combine visual and tactile qualities of materials and processes and to match these qualities to the purpose of the work.

c) use a variety of methods and approaches to communicate observations, ideas and feelings, and to design and make images and artefacts.

### Unit 5: Breadth of study

During the key stage, pupils should be taught the knowledge, skills and understanding through:

▶ ▶ ▶

a) exploring a range of starting points for practical work, for example, themselves, their experiences, images, stories, drama, music, natural and made objects and environments.

b) working on their own, and collaborating with others, on projects in two and three dimensions and on different scales.

c) using a range of materials and processes, including ICT, for example, painting, collage, print making, digital media, textiles, sculpture.

d) investigating art, craft and design in the locality and in a variety of genres, styles and traditions, for example, in original and reproduction form, during visits to museums, galleries and sites, on the Internet.

### Make a frieze

Make a frieze to tell the story of Easter. Research the ways in which other artists have told parts of the story in art, such as Leonardo da Vinci's *The Last Supper*. Research the Internet or local churches to find examples of the Stations of the Cross. See the Bibliography on page 79 for more information. The finished frieze could be displayed around the performance room or used as a backdrop for the set.

## Story in pictures

Select one or more Bible passages listed in the 'Scene synopsis' chapter on page 10. The children could look at ways of telling stories in pictures, such as comic strips, cartoons and storyboards. Tell the children to look at the story and work out what elements they should include.

Alternatively, the children could make individual backdrops for each scene or a generic one that could be used for all five scenes.

## Publicity

In groups, the children could think about ideas for designing the cover of the programme, as well as making posters, tickets and a logo for the play (all with ICT links).

## Face painting

It would be helpful to think about make-up and how it could be used in the performance. The children could draw the faces of the main characters on to sheets of paper and show their ideas for make-up. The ideas could then be translated into reality by experimenting with face paints, either by practising making up the actors for the play or by working in pairs to try out their ideas on each other.

# Information and communication technology (ICT)

## INFORMATION AND COMMUNICATION TECHNOLOGY

(Key Stage 2)

### Unit 1: Finding things out

Pupils should be taught how to:

a) gather information from a variety of sources.

### Unit 2: Developing ideas and making things happen

Pupils should be taught to:

a) use text, tables, images and sound to develop their ideas.

### Unit 3: Exchanging and sharing information

Pupils should be taught how to:

a) share their ideas by presenting information in a variety of forms.
b) present their completed work effectively.

## Media and computer technology

When we performed the play in the field test, we tried to use lots of different types of media and computer technology. First of all, we prerecorded the introduction to the play. As this was read, we projected images, using a data-projector, on to a screen behind the stage. The images were produced using PowerPoint software. This technique could be repeated at various points in the play as desired.

For Scene 4, we recorded some footage of a cross on a hill, using a video camera, and played it as the meditations were read out and as the solo song was sung.

### Image projection

To find images suitable for projection, the children could search the Internet using a search engine such as 'Google' (which has an image search). Images could also been scanned in. Source material could include images that children have drawn themselves, or pictures from books and magazines.

Children could also use digital cameras to photograph images. Suitable images could include a cross, market scenes, or a hill.

Video cameras could be used to film a market place or to create a montage for the crucifixion scene. The resulting footage could be projected during the performance. You may wish to delegate a child to be in charge of shooting the whole play on a video camera. Children could also video some of the rehearsals and preparation time to make a video diary of the event.

## Designing the programme

Computer design packages could be used to produce the layout for the inside of the programme, using the material developed in English and art and design (see pages 25 and 29).

## Breadth of study

ICT spans many other curriculum subjects and you will find further suggestions using ICT in the links for art and design, design technology, English and RE.

# Music

**MUSIC**

(Key Stage 2)

### Unit 1: Controlling sound through singing and playing—performing skills

Pupils should be taught to:

a) sing songs, in unison and two parts, with clear diction, control of pitch, a sense of phrase and musical expression.
b) play tuned and untuned instruments with control and rhythmic accuracy.
c) practise, rehearse and present performances with an awareness of the audience.

*This Man Called Jesus* provides links into the programme of study for music through the songs. To this end, musical skills are explored through vocal exercises and suggestions for learning the songs themselves.

Taking part in group singing is a bit like being involved in a sports team. First of all, it is important always to warm up your voice to avoid damaging your vocal chords. Second, it is important to remember to work together to produce a good sound. Below are a few exercises to help prepare the voice for singing.

## Warm-up exercises

Ask the children to find their own space in the room or hall, so that they can stretch without bumping into anyone else. When they are ready, tell them to stand with their feet slightly apart, so that they are balanced and relaxed. Then give the following instructions.

1. Slowly tense your whole body, starting with your toes and moving all the way up your body to your head. Then, equally slowly, relax again.
2. Wiggle your fingers, and then let the wiggle travel all the way through your body until you are shaking like a jelly.
3. Stretch up high in the air and then relax.
4. Roll your shoulders gently backwards and then roll them gently forwards.

## Mouth exercises

When you are singing, it is very important that the words can be heard. A gymnast has to be very precise in their movements so that the movement fits to the music. A singer has to be equally precise in fitting the words to the music.

To warm up the children's mouth muscles ready for singing, give the following instructions:

1. Make lots of different emotions with your face and mouth. Particularly, use big smiles and sad faces in order to stretch and relax the face muscles.
2. Think about the mouth shape needed for each vowel sound. Try saying phrases such as 'How now brown cow', or sound sequences such as 'May me my mow moo' to help with this.
3. Pronounce consonants clearly, especially at the end of a sentence or phrase. Try singing 'Dad's got a head like a ping-pong ball' to the tune of *The William Tell Overture*, making sure that the 'P's are very clear (try putting your hand in front of your mouth and feel the air shoot on to your hand when you sing a 'P' sound).

## Breathing exercises

To prepare the children's breathing for singing, give the following instructions.

1. Breathe in through your nose, imagining that you are a hot-air balloon and that you are expanding

with air. As you do this, make sure that you're not making a sound or raising your shoulders. Then breathe the air out through your mouth. Note: this is a relaxing exercise for breathing: pupils should ideally breathe through the mouth when singing. Try adding a note when breathing out, and see how long you can sing it for.

2. Imagine that you are silently drinking a pint of cold air in one draught. Can you feel the cold air on the back of your throat? If you can, then you are breathing in correctly.

3. Imagine that your throat is a big cave when you breathe in, and that when you sing a note the cave makes an echoing sound.

4. Take a breath and then walk slowly around the room, breathing out as you move. When the air runs out, take another breath and change direction. Gradually add a different sound to the air you're breathing out, such as 'sss', 'aah', 'eeh', 'ooh', 'umm' and so on.

## Rhythm, pitch and dynamics

To improve rhythm, pitch and dynamics, try the following suggestions.

1. Ask the group to sit in a circle. Practise clapping a rhythm such as: knee, knee, clap, rest. Go round the circle clapping this rhythm, with children taking it in turns to say their name in the rhythm. Extend

the exercise by asking them to try saying their name using a wide range from high to low, from fast to slow and so on.

2. To practise dynamics, start by making a 'sshh' sound. Ask children to follow your direction, so that when you put your hand up they get louder and when you put your hand down they get quieter. Extend the exercise by asking the children to take it in turns to conduct. You could repeat this exercise using notes instead of the 'sshh' sound. As you move from high to low, get the children to follow the height of the music with their own hands.

3. To practise pitch, sing a note and then ask the group to do an action, such as clapping, jumping in the air, touching their toes or spinning around. When they have completed the action, ask them to sing the note you sang. Extend the exercise by singing groups of notes followed by an action. Alternatively, ask one of the children to be the teacher and sing the note(s).

## Singing exercises

To practise singing scales, sing them to phrases such as 'chocolate cheesecake' or 'My car has a flat tyre' (below).

Finally, you could also sing a few familiar songs or rounds (such as Frère Jacques or London's Burning). Other suggestions can be found in the Bibliography on page 79. When you have completed a range of exercises as outlined above, you will be ready to sing.

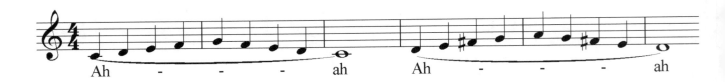

## Learning the songs

With each song, start by learning the rhythm of the words. Say a line in the right rhythm and then ask the children to repeat it. When you have practised this, add the music by asking the children to hum just the tune without words. Then put the two together. Extend this exercise by playing the tune to the children, but stopping at a random point. Do they know which word you've finished on?

## Jesus is coming/Jesus is living

Explore the ideas in these two songs: for example, march in time around the room, clapping on the second and fourth beats. Sing each section of the song three or four times in a row before moving on.

## We want rid of him

Ask the children to find all the rhyming words in the song. This is an angry song, so suggest that the children sing it in an angry and nasty way, making an emphasis on the word 'Jesus' at the end of each verse. Shakers would work well in this song, as would stringed instruments if you have any string players in your group.

## Why do we call it Good Friday?

Divide the song into three sections. Learn the melody with the children singing 'lah' or 'ah'. Ask them to move their hands up and down to the pitch of the melody. Add chime bars, playing on the notes indicated by the chords above the music. Add recorders.

## Barabbas' song

This song is intended to be performed as a solo, so if you have a child who is able and willing to sing a solo, they will need a bit of time on their own to practise it. All the children could join in the chorus.

## Clap your hands, shout hallelujah

Learn the chorus. First of all, learn the rhythm, which is used all the way through the song. Keep repeating the phrase 'Clap your hands' in the correct rhythm. Some of the children could play percussion instruments with this rhythm at the same time.

## CURRICULUM LINK

### Unit 2: Creating and developing musical ideas—composing skills

Pupils should be taught to:

a) improvise, developing rhythmic and melodic material when performing.
b) explore, choose, combine and organize musical ideas within musical structures.

Although there is no suggested incidental music included in the play, the children could be encouraged to compose musical interludes for use between scenes or to describe certain moments. Children could then notate their compositions in scores, using pictures or diagrams or manuscript notation, and perform them as part of the play, either live or prerecorded.

## CURRICULUM LINK

### Unit 4: Listening, and applying knowledge and understanding

Pupils should be taught:

b) how the combined musical elements of pitch, duration, dynamics, tempo, timbre, texture and silence can be organized within musical structures and used to communicate different moods and effects.

Many composers over the centuries have written music depicting the story of Holy Week and Easter. Have available a selection of well-known works and ask the children to listen to how the story is portrayed in the music. Examples could include the following.

## Handel

Listen to the Hallelujah Chorus from *Messiah*.

❖ How does the music make you feel?
❖ What part of the story of Jesus' life is the composer expressing?
❖ How has he created the feeling of joy in the music?

## Bach

Listen to the Passion Chorale, 'O sacred head, sore wounded'. This piece expresses the emotions felt at the death of Jesus. Ask the children to draw pictures as they listen, thinking about the part of the story that this music is telling: the death and burial of Jesus.

❖ Compare and contrast this piece with the Hallelujah Chorus.
❖ What techniques has the composer used to express the sadness of the story?
❖ How does the music make you feel?

## CURRICULUM LINK

### Unit 5: Breadth of study

Pupils should be taught knowledge, skills and understanding through:

e) a range of live and recorded music from different times and cultures.

Other music you could listen to includes *Godspell* by John-Michael Tebelak, Stainer's *Crucifixion* and hymns or songs used today in church worship (see Bibliography on page 79 for suggestions).

**SECTION THREE**

# RE links

# Who was Jesus?

In October 2004 the QCA published a non-statutory national framework for the teaching of religious education. The following links are based on the units for Key Stage 2 in that document.

---

### UNIT 1: LEARNING ABOUT RELIGION

Pupils should be taught to:

a) describe the key aspects of religions, especially the people, stories and traditions that influence the beliefs and values of others.

g) use religious language in communicating their knowledge and understanding.

h) use and interpret information about religion from a range of sources.

---

Brainstorm with the children what they already know about Jesus. You could display these answers and refer back to them after performing the play to see if (and in what way) their answers have changed.

Carry out a hot-seating exercise with the different characters in the play, to build up a picture of what the other people in the story thought about Jesus. Extend the exercise by asking the children to report the outcome of the hot-seating to the group in a variety of ways, such as writing newspaper reports, interviewing each other or drawing and painting pictures. Ask if there are any particular words describing Jesus that occur more than once.

Have a discussion about what Jesus' enemies thought of him. As well as those who were obviously plotting against Jesus, think about those who could be considered as enemies of Jesus before they met him, such as Zacchaeus. Children could also look at the way some characters' opinions of Jesus changed when they got to know him better (such as Zacchaeus or the thief on the cross).

On the next two pages is a list of characters and some Bible references that link to them. Explain that almost everything we know about Jesus comes from the Bible. Ask the children to look up some of the Bible references and put themselves in that character's shoes. As all the references come from the four Gospels, it may be helpful to provide individual Gospels or copies of the New Testament. Alternatively, you may wish to carry out some of the research online.

Ask the children to imagine how these characters really felt about Jesus. What did they see Jesus doing? Would they have been scared of Jesus or amazed by him? Would they have been jealous or proud to know him? Try to get the actors in the group to look at the characters they are playing themselves, and suggest that they either write something about the way that character felt or work in pairs—one as the interviewer and one as the character. Compile a list of questions that they could ask, such as 'When and where did you first meet Jesus? What did you think of him then? 'Did your feelings about him change? Are you any different now from when you first met Jesus?'

You could also invite a Christian into school to talk about their own experience. Many Christians will have a testimony to tell about how they came to know Jesus.

Children could put together a fact file or curriculum vitae for Jesus. They could include when and where he was born, what his occupation was, what his gifts were, when and where he died, why he died, how he described himself. Some children could write references for Jesus either from one of the disciples' points of view or the point of view of Pilate or Caiaphas.

## Judas Iscariot

Disciple and betrayer of Jesus.

Matthew 10:4; Mark 3:19; Luke 6:16
John 6:71; 12:4
Matthew 26:14–56; Mark 14:10–50; Luke 22:3–53; John 13:2–30
John 18:2–11
Matthew 27:3–5
Acts 1:16–25

## Peter

Also known as Simon. Disciple of Jesus and author of 1 and 2 Peter.

Matthew 10:2; Mark 3:16
Matthew 16:13–20; Mark 8:27–30; Luke 9:18–21
Matthew 17:1–8; Mark 9:2–8; Luke 9:28–36; 2 Peter 1:16–18
Matthew 17:24–27
Matthew 26:31–35; Mark 14:27–31; Luke 22:31–34; John 13:31–38
Matthew 26:69–75; Mark 14:66–72; Luke 22:54–62; John 18:15–27
John 21:15–23

## James

Disciple of Jesus. Son of Zebedee and brother of John.

Matthew 4:21–22; Luke 5:1–10
Mark 3:17; Matthew 10:2
Matthew 17:1–13; Mark 9:1–13; Luke 9:28–36
Mark 10:35–45
Acts 12:2

## John

Disciple of Jesus. Son of Zebedee, brother of James, author of 1, 2, 3 John and (traditionally) Revelation.

Matthew 4:21–22; Luke 5:1–10
Mark 3:17; Matthew 10:2
Matthew 17:1–13; Mark 9:1–13; Luke 9:28–36
Mark 10:35–45
Acts 4:1–3
Revelation 1:1–3, 9
Revelation 22:8

## Thomas

Disciple of Jesus.

Matthew 10:3; Mark 3:18; Luke 6:15

John 11:16
John 14:5
John 21:2
Acts 1:13
John 20:24–28

## Andrew

Disciple of Jesus.

Matthew 4:18; Mark 1:16–18, 29
Mark 3:18; John 1:35–44
Luke 6:14
Matthew 10:2
John 6:8–9
Mark 13:3
John 12:22
Acts 1:13

## Barabbas

Criminal who had started a riot in the city of Jerusalem and committed murder.

Matthew 27:15–26

## Pilate

Governor of Judea and Samaria at the time of Jesus.

John 18—19
Matthew 27
Mark 15
Luke 22—23

## Pharisees

One of the two main religious parties within Judaism in New Testament times.

Matthew 5:20; 16:6; 23:13

## Caiaphas

The Jewish high priest in Jerusalem during the time of Jesus.

Matthew 26:3
John 11:47–53
Matthew 26:57–68
Mark 14:53–65
John 18:12–14, 19–24
Luke 3:2

## Servant girls

Members of the household of the high priest, Caiaphas.

Mark 14:66–72

## Mary Magdalene

A follower of Jesus.

Mark 15:40–41; 16:1, 9
Luke 8:2; 24:10
Matthew 27:56
John 19:25; 20:1–2

## Salome

A follower of Jesus. Commonly believed to have been the mother of James and John and the wife of Zebedee.

Mark 15:40–41
Mark 16:1
Matthew 27:56

## Malchus

One of the high priest's servants. During Jesus' arrest, Peter struck at him with a sword, cutting off his ear. Jesus subsequently healed him.

Matthew 26:50–54
John 18:10
Luke 22:49–51

## Accusers

Members of the crowd at the time of Jesus' trial.

Luke 23:1–5
Matthew 26:59–63
Mark 14:53–59

# Why is Easter important to Christians?

Again, the following links are based on the units for Key Stage 2 in the non-statutory national framework for the teaching of religious education published in October 2004.

---

## UNIT 2: LEARNING FROM RELIGION

Pupils should be taught to:

a) discuss their own and others' views of religious truth and belief, expressing their own ideas clearly.

b) reflect on issues of right and wrong and their own and others' responses to them.

c) reflect on sources of inspiration in their own and others' lives.

---

Because *This Man Called Jesus* tells the story of Holy Week and Easter, from the triumphant entry to Jerusalem to the resurrection and ascension, it provides an ideal platform to help the children experience and understand the story for themselves through rehearsing and performing the play. In this way, children will be able to experience the story by being involved. Below is a list of suggestions to help build on the experience of being involved in the play.

## Scene 1: Jesus enters Jerusalem (Palm Sunday)

Read the account of Palm Sunday in Matthew 21:1–17, or read through the first page of the script (page 51).

There are two parts to be considered in this story. First of all, we see the excitement of the crowd. They welcome Jesus as he rides into Jerusalem on a donkey, believing him to be the long-awaited king who would rescue them from Roman occupation. The second thing to consider is the fact that Jesus knew he was entering Jerusalem to die.

In order to compare and contrast the ideas of Jesus being hailed as a king and Jesus coming to die, ask two children to dress up—one as a king (wearing crown and royal robes, riding into Jerusalem on a donkey) and one as Jesus ready to die (wearing a crown of thorns, a purple robe and carrying a heavy cross). Compare the words the crowd shouted as Jesus entered Jerusalem (Matthew 21:9) with those shouted at his trial (Matthew 27:20–23).

Ask the children to think of someone they admire, such as a football player, a pop star or an actor. Imagine that that person was coming into your neighbourhood. How would you react? What would you do? How would you feel? The people of Jerusalem reacted a bit like this when Jesus arrived. They spread their cloaks on the ground and waved palm branches as a sign of respect for Jesus.

Then ask the children to imagine that they've decided they no longer like that person, for whatever reason. How would they react now? Talk about the huge change in the people's reactions to Jesus.

Jesus rode into Jerusalem on a donkey. Why did he do that? Read Zechariah 9:9 in the Old Testament. This passage was written many years before Jesus was born. Christians believe that this is a sign pointing to Jesus as the Messiah—the one promised by God.

## Scene 2: The last meal together

Read the account of the last supper in Luke 22:7–34, or read through the script of Scene 2 in the play (page 53). Explore the following themes:

❖ Passover: You will find information about Passover under the heading 'Bread and wine' on page 46.

❖ Promise: Talk about Peter's promise never to leave Jesus. Find out about how and why he broke this promise by reading Luke 22:54–62. Talk about making promises.

## Scene 3: The garden of Gethsemane

Read the account of the garden of Gethsemane and Jesus' trial in Matthew 26:36–68 and 27:11–26, or read through the script of Scene 3 in the play (page 54). Why did Jesus go to Gethsemane? What did he pray? Why was it important for the disciples to stay awake? What happened to the disciples? How do you think Jesus felt when he found the disciples asleep? Have you ever felt disappointed with someone?

Find a team game to play with the children to show the importance of working together (for example, see the Bibliography, page 80: *Theme Games* by Lesley Pinchbeck).

Discuss how Jesus' friends behaved in negative ways towards Jesus. Consider the character of Judas. Was he always an enemy of Jesus? Why did he decide to betray Jesus? Look at the words of the song 'We want rid of him'. Discuss how the song helps your understanding of Judas' decision. How did Judas feel after he had betrayed Jesus? Read the account of what happened next in Matthew 27:1–10. Do you think Jesus would have forgiven Judas if he had said sorry?

Read the account of Peter's denial in Matthew 26:69–75. Why did Peter say that he didn't know Jesus? Jesus had said that this would happen. What does this show about Jesus? How do you think Peter felt when he realized what he had said? Have you ever said things you shouldn't have? How did you feel afterwards? How do you think Jesus would have felt about Peter? To find out how the story of Peter's denial ends, read the account in John 21:15–19.

## Scene 4: The crucifixion

It is sometimes helpful to consider the crucifixion from the point of view of a bystander who was present at the time. Historically, many meditations have been written from the viewpoint of people such as the man who made the nails, or Simon of Cyrene, who carried the cross for Jesus. In the play, Barabbas' viewpoint is used to help the children understand more fully the sacrifice that Jesus made in taking someone's place. Christians believe that Jesus took the place of all humankind when he submitted himself to death on the cross, and putting ourselves in Barabbas' shoes gives us an insight into what that means.

Scene 4 has been left unscripted deliberately, to give the children an opportunity to contribute their own creative input to the play. The intention is that children read out some of their own poems, songs, letters and diary entries written from Barabbas' point of view, based on class work undertaken during the preparation time. Alternatively, one child could read out a compilation of all or some of the children's work. Images of the cross could be projected on to a screen at the back of stage. These images could be created using video, slides or montage (see ICT suggestions on page 31). The child who is playing Barabbas could recite some of the contribution or, if preferred, he or she could sit silently (in character) in the middle of the stage while someone else reads the contributions.

Below are some examples of creative writing that explore the events of Jesus' trial and death from Barabbas' point of view. Some of the pieces are the work of a Year 4 class; others are a compilation of the children's work used in the original performance.

## How did Barabbas feel?

I felt unhappy when I was put in the wet smelly prison. When I was put in the prison I had some metal loops put on my legs and arms. There was a little window with some metal bars. I was about to be put on the cross for murdering someone when I heard some people saying my name and shouting, 'Release him' and 'Put Jesus on the cross instead.' I felt really sad because of all the good things Jesus had done. Someone came and unlocked the cell and said that he was coming to release me because Jesus is coming to take my place on the cross.

All I felt was guilt. I thought of Jesus in my head. Why? What had happened to make him take my place? I felt really worried and scared. I just did not know why he wanted to take my place and sacrifice himself for me. But at the same time I felt relieved that it wasn't me. Why didn't Jesus fight back? I should be on that cross.

Jesus took my place even though he did nothing wrong. I felt sorry for him. I am going to do what Jesus told everyone to do.

## Barabbas

As I sat in my cold, dark, damp prison cell wishing upon wishes that I hadn't killed that man, I began to hear what sounded like a very large crowd shouting. As the shouting grew louder and more agitated, I realized that they were shouting MY name! My name!! 'Release Barabbas, release Barabbas, release Barabbas,' they cried! But why? I'd committed murder. I was due to be killed that very day!

There were three crosses ready for the three criminals to be crucified that day—one was meant for me!

'Nail him to a cross! Nail him to a cross!' I heard the crowd shout. 'Nail who to a cross?' I asked myself. 'If they want me released, who are they going to crucify?' The noise from outside grew louder and louder and the shouts of 'Nail him to a cross!' grew even more persistent.

Finally, when the shouting became almost deafening, a cheer erupted, and then I began to hear my name again, 'Barabbas, Barabbas, Barabbas…'

My mind was filled with emotion. I wasn't sure what was happening. Just then a guard came in and unlocked the chains I was in and said, 'You are free to go. Jesus is going to be put to death in your place.'

'Jesus? Why? What's he done wrong?' I asked.

'Nothing that deserves death!'

'Then I should die, not him.'

'Well, yes! But the crowd wanted to see Jesus die and you freed!'

I couldn't believe my ears—I was a free man! I'd been given a second chance! Jesus was to die in my place! Why didn't Jesus put up a fight? It was as if he knew it was meant to happen!

## Jesus took my place

**J**esus took my place.
**E**very night until this day I waited to die but Jesus took my place.
**S**urprised that I was released.
**U**nhappy because I liked Jesus.
**S**orry for the things I did wrong.

BY MARTIN

## Jesus died on the cross

**J**esus died on the cross.
**E**veryone cheered.
**S**ome felt sorry.
**U**ntil in the end our
**S**aviour rose again.

BY KATIE

## Christ was crucified

**C**hrist was crucified,
**R**eleasing me, I
**U**nderstood why
**C**hrist rose again
**I**n every country for Christians,
**F**reeing us all,
**Y**oung and old.

BY RAHUL

## Dear Zoe,

I felt saddened and upset when they told me Jesus was going to die for me. Suddenly I heard a crowd shout, 'Kill him, kill him.' I was standing at the window, pulling on the bars. Then I remembered that Jesus was going to die for me and that he would possibly rise again. All of a sudden I didn't feel so guilty. I could not rise again, could I? My guilt suddenly lessened.

BY KIESHA

## I would feel sad

I would feel sad because Jesus is getting killed.

FROM ANISA

## Dear Diary

Today is my last night in prison. I can't stop thinking of Jesus. I feel quite sad and guilty, but at the same time relieved that it won't be me. Why didn't Jesus fight back? I don't understand. I should be on that cross.

BY TASHIEKA

43

## Barabbas

**B**arabbas felt shocked: in a way he thought Jesus knew what was going to happen.

**A**mazed: Barabbas thought Jesus was going to come back alive.

**R**ealized: Barabbas was very puzzled because Jesus had done nothing wrong.

**A**ppalled: people in the crowd shouted to release Barabbas.

**B**lamed: Jesus didn't shout or scream even though he was going to die.

**B**rush with death: Barabbas was free but Jesus took his place.

**A**ngry: Barabbas thought he was going to die.

**S**aved: Barabbas didn't know how to thank Jesus.

BY THOMAS C

## I was sat lonely

I was sat lonely, on my own in my cell. All I felt was guilt. I thought of Jesus in my head. Why? What had happened to make him take my place? I felt really worried and scared. I just did not know why he wanted to take my place and sacrifice himself for me. I thought it would be the last day of my life, but it wasn't.

BY JACK

## Barabbas

**B**ad
**A**mazed
**R**eleased
**A**stonished
**B**lamed
**B**rave
**A**ngry
**S**urprised

BY JAMES

## Dear Diary

I don't know why, but people wanted Jesus to die instead of me. I should have died because I did wrong. But what if they just want to know if he is God's son? Well, so do I, but friends believe each other. If he does die and go on the cross, I know that he will come back! No one else has to believe he will. And why isn't Jesus putting up a fight? Why, why do people want him to die? Well, I know he's a good man, but I should die as well. But if I do I won't come alive like Jesus will.

BY JADE

## Came to take Barabbas' place

**C**ame to take Barabbas' place.
**R**eleased from jail.
**U**nhappy that Jesus was going to die and
**C**rucified on the cross.
**I**nterested in what was happening.
**F**illed with horror.
**Y**earning for freedom.

BY LUKE

## I was in prison

I was in prison and I was about to get put on the cross for murdering someone. I heard some people saying my name and shouting 'Release him' and 'Put Jesus on the cross instead.' I felt really sad because of all the nice things Jesus had done. Someone came and unlocked the cage and said that he was coming to release me because Jesus was coming to take my place on the cross. I felt really sad. I felt confused. It should have been me on that cross. Crucify me! Crucify me!

BY THOMAS G

## Jesus is going to be killed

**J** Jesus is going to be killed.
**E** Everyone wants him to be dead.
**S** Soon he was killed.
**U** Unbelievable, thought Barabbas when he realized he was going to be free.
**S** Barabbas was excited because he was saved.

BY KIRSTY

## Barabbas lesson plan

The account of the release of Barabbas can be found in the three synoptic Gospels: Luke 23:1–25; Mark 15:1–15 and Matthew 27:15–26. The following lesson plan is based on the account in Luke's Gospel.

**Exercise 1**: As a class, read the story of Barabbas in Luke 23:1–25. Lead into a discussion about what the story says, using the questions suggested below.

❖ What had Barabbas done wrong, to be sentenced to death? (v. 19).

❖ What was the charge against Jesus? (vv. 2–4 and vv. 13–26. See also Luke 20:20–26).

❖ Why had the guards and the chief priests brought Jesus to Pilate? (vv. 1–2).

❖ Why did Pilate release Barabbas? (vv. 24–25; see also Matthew 27:15).

❖ How do you think Barabbas felt, knowing that Jesus was going to take his place and die?

❖ Do you think Jesus deserved to take Barabbas' place? Why? Why not?

**Exercise 2**: Ask the children to imagine they are Barabbas and consider these questions.

❖ What sort of words would you use to describe how you feel when you hear the crowds shouting for you to be freed and for Jesus to take your place?

❖ Would you change the way you live your life after you were freed? In what ways would you change?

❖ What are your thoughts about Jesus?

**Exercise 3**: As Barabbas, you have been given one piece of paper and a pencil to write down your feelings about what has happened. You could write a letter home or a diary entry. You may want to write a poem or a song. You could write an acrostic poem using the word 'Barabbas' or 'Jesus' or 'Crucify'.

Once the children have completed the task, you could link the exercise to ICT by asking them to type their work up. You could then include some of their poems and letters in the programme for the performance, which some of the children could design on the computer.

See pages 42–44 for examples of work based on this exercise. Read these examples to the children to help spark ideas before they begin their work.

Prepare by wrapping an empty box in gift paper and attaching a card saying, 'Dear (your name), happy Easter, love from God.' Present the box to the class. Build up the expectation of the children by asking them what they think might be in the box. Unwrap the box, keeping up the air of expectation. When the box is unwrapped, tip it upside down and show that there is nothing inside. Ask the children what they think this means. Then begin to talk about the story of how Jesus' body was laid in the tomb after he had died and how, on the first Easter Sunday, three days after Jesus had died, the women went to the tomb and found that it was empty—just like the box.

Ask the children to imagine what the women would have thought. Had the body been stolen? But there had been soldiers guarding the tomb and a huge stone placed in front of it.

What was the reaction of the disciples when they heard what had happened? Jesus appeared to the disciples when they were gathered behind the locked doors of the upper room. He showed them his wounds. How would you have reacted if you had been a disciple? Would you have believed that Jesus had come back to life?

Explain that even though the box was empty, just as the tomb was empty, this gift represents the best present that God has ever given—because Christians believe that Jesus rose from the dead. They believe that through his resurrection Jesus conquered death by bringing life after death to those who believe in him. Remind the children that the story doesn't end with Jesus rising to new life, but that he went back to his Father in heaven. Christians believe that when we die we will join Jesus in heaven, just as he has promised (see Matthew 26:29) and that he will always be with us (Matthew 28:20).

Ask the children to think of something amazing they've seen, such as a concert, a film or someone breaking a world record. Would they keep what they'd seen to themselves? Then ask them to imagine what it must have felt like to see Jesus after he had come back to life. Would they want to keep that news to themselves? Talk about how Jesus told his disciples to go and tell everyone what they had seen, and how Christians believe that Jesus meant for everyone who believes in him to go and tell others about him.

## Scene 5: The resurrection

Read the account of the resurrection in Matthew 28, or read through the script of Scene 5 in the play (pages 57–59).

# Learning about symbols

Pupils should be taught the knowledge, skills and understanding through:

h) symbols and religious expression: how religious and spiritual ideas are expressed.

There are many signs and symbols in the Christian faith. The particular symbols and signs that relate to *This Man Called Jesus* are bread and wine and the cross.

## Bread and wine

Read the account of the last supper in Luke 22:7–34, or read through the script of Scene 2 in the play (page 53). What does Jesus say that the bread and the wine represent? Why does he say this?

Begin to talk about sacrifice. One dictionary definition is 'giving up something valued for the sake of anything or anyone else, especially a higher good'. From earliest times people expressed their devotion to God through presenting to him offerings as a sign of thanks and fellowship, or for the forgiveness of sins. In the latter case, the sacrifice of a slaughtered animal symbolized the bearing of the penalty in a person's stead. Christians believe that Christ sacrificed his life on the cross to pay the penalty for the sins of humankind. Talk about how sacrifice can mean taking the blame for something someone else has done. As a visual example, you could show the part of the film *The Lion King* where Mufasa gives his life to save his son Simba.

Read about the events of the Passover in the Old Testament. The story can be found in Exodus 6—14, but particularly in chapters 11 and 12. The name of the festival recalls the act of God 'passing over' the houses of the Israelites when the final Egyptian plague took place—that of the killing of the firstborn son of every

Egyptian family. God withheld judgment from the Israelite households only when he saw the blood of the sacrificial lamb around the front door, showing that an innocent life had been taken in place of the one under judgment. Talk about what this must have been like for the Israelites, and explain about the festival of Passover, which celebrates the Israelites' miraculous escape from Egypt. The Passover meal is still celebrated today by those who follow Judaism. You could have your own Passover meal in the classroom (see Bibliography on page 79 for resources).

By the time of Jesus, the festival of Passover had developed into a set form with a number of added rituals. Among the additions to the meal was a cup of wine, for which the head of the household offered a prayer of thanks both before and after the eating of the unleavened bread. Explain that when Jesus and his friends met in the upper room to eat their final meal together, they were meeting to celebrate the Passover. The bread and wine that Jesus used to symbolize his death would have been a normal part of the meal. Jesus knew that he was now the Passover lamb, laying down his innocent life in place of those under judgment. Once Jesus had died, Christians replaced the festival of Passover with a new celebration of remembrance—the Lord's Supper, which is also known as Mass or Holy Communion. The service of Holy Communion is a symbolic way in which Christians remember Jesus' words at the last supper and his subsequent death and resurrection.

If any of the children attend a church, ask them how their church celebrates Holy Communion. You could visit a local church and ask the minister to show the children what happens during Holy Communion. Ask him or her to show the children the prayers that are said in this special service. There are also a number of books that help children to understand what Holy Communion is about (see Bibliography on page 80 for more details).

## The cross

The story of Jesus' crucifixion can be found in all four of the Gospels: Matthew 27:31–56; Mark 15:20–41; Luke 23:26–49; John 19:16–37. To the Gospel writers, the story of Jesus' death upon the cross was the central point in the story of salvation. The cross therefore became a symbol for the salvation of all humankind. In New Testament times, crucifixion was a form of torture and execution used by the Romans. (The Jewish authorities were under the rule of Rome, and had no power themselves to carry out execution.) Although the Gospel writers refer to the cruelty and injustice of Jesus' crucifixion, their main concern is not with the physical horror of his death but with its theological meaning.

Read through one or more of the accounts of Jesus' crucifixion with the children, or watch it on video, using a film such as *The Miracle Maker* or *Jesus of Nazareth* (the latter has a PG certificate). Ask the children why they think the cross is an important symbol for Christians. Link the discussion back to the concept of sacrifice outlined above. What does the cross remind Christians of? Where can you find the symbol of the cross today? Why do people wear crosses, make a sign of the cross or display the cross in windows or on churches?

# This Man Called Jesus: full script

# This Man Called Jesus

## JESUS ENTERS JERUSALEM

###  Cast

- ❖ Narrators 1, 2, 3, 4 and 5
- ❖ Crowd
- ❖ Thomas
- ❖ Andrew
- ❖ Mary
- ❖ Salome
- ❖ Other disciples
- ❖ Accusers
- ❖ Josephus
- ❖ Gaius
- ❖ Orpah
- ❖ Jesus
- ❖ Chief priests 1, 2 and 3
- ❖ Girl with a bottle of perfume
- ❖ Judas Iscariot

###  Props

- ❖ Recording of opening narration on CD or cassette (optional)
- ❖ Projection screen (optional)
- ❖ Video player, slide projector or data projector and laptop with PowerPoint for a static display or montage (all optional)

###  Songs

- ❖ Jesus is coming
- ❖ We want rid of him

**Narrator 1:** We've been following the story of this man called Jesus. This is the story so far. He was born in a stable, grew into a fine young man, and seems to be someone quite special. He has performed many miracles, told lots of stories, and gained many friends and followers, including twelve special friends, known as his disciples. His friends and followers have realized that he's special: in fact, this man called Jesus is the Son of God. They are all on a journey to Jerusalem, and Jesus has just told his friends that while they are there he is going to die. They are horrified by this news and don't really know what to think. Some are amazed, some are afraid, and some just don't understand. He's told them lots of stories to try to prepare them for what's going to happen, but nothing could quite prepare them for what happened next.

*Music: Jesus is coming*

*Enter children carrying palm branches.*

**Narrator 1:** So we join this man called Jesus and his disciples as they are about to enter Jerusalem. Everyone has heard that Jesus is on his way, and they're all very excited. They can't wait to meet him! It is an amazing sight: many people are on the road, waving branches and spreading their cloaks on the ground as Jesus passes by, riding on a donkey. They're singing and shouting at the tops of their voices.

*Song: Jesus is coming*

**Andrew:** Hosanna! Hosanna!
**Mary:** Blessed is he who comes in the name of the Lord!

**Salome:** Hosanna in the highest!
**Narrator 1:** So Jesus and his disciples approached Jerusalem to a huge welcome. By the time they entered into the city, it was getting dark. Everyone was asking, 'Who can this be?
**Thomas:** This is Jesus, the prophet from Nazareth in Galilee.

*Enter the enemies of Jesus stage right (the market place).*

**Narrator 4:** The next morning, Jesus went to the temple, where he saw people buying and selling animals and birds in the temple forecourt. The temple was God's holy place: a house of prayer.
**Josephus:** Come and get your sacrifices here! Going cheap today. A fresh male goat at half price!
**Gaius:** How much for a pair of doves, mate?
**Orpah:** Have you got any pigeons?

*Enter Jesus stage left.*

**Narrator 2:** Now Jesus wasn't happy when he saw what was taking place. In fact, he was very angry—so angry that he turned over all the tables, creating complete chaos, scattering animals and sending birds flying. No one could sell anything after that. He said to them…
**Jesus:** The Scriptures say, 'My house should be called a place of worship. But you have turned it into a place where robbers hide.'

*Exit Jesus stage left.*

**Narrator 3:** People were amazed by what Jesus said. Most of them realized that he was right. But a few—the chief priests and religious leaders—were very unhappy about his actions and started to plot against him.

Reproduced with permission from *This Man Called Jesus* published by BRF 2005 (1 84101 434 6) www.barnabasinschools.org.uk

**Chief priest 1:** They're listening to him instead of us. What can we do?

**Chief priest 2:** We need to get rid of him—trick him into doing something wrong.

**Chief priest 1:** Maybe we can get one of his disciples on our side. We could give him some money. What do you think?

**Narrator 2:** So they carried on plotting how they could trick Jesus into doing something wrong or saying something against the law, and they came up with the plan.

*Jesus and disciples enter stage left.*

**Narrator 5:** The very next day, Jesus was walking through the temple with his disciples when the chief priests and religious leaders came up to him and asked…

**Chief priest 1:** Who are you? Who said you could speak like this to our people?

**Narrator 2:** But Jesus knew what they were trying to do, and said to them that if they answered one of his questions first, then he would answer theirs. They didn't know the answer to his question, so he didn't have to answer theirs.

**Narrator 4:** After this, Jesus started to teach the people about God by telling stories. He told one about people who were looking after a vineyard for the owner—and doing it badly. The chief priests knew that Jesus was talking about them, and this made them even more determined to get rid of him. But people were flocking around Jesus, and the chief priests were unable to do anything. They just kept on trying to trick Jesus, asking him all sorts of hard questions—but he always came up with the right answer.

**Chief priest 2:** Teacher, should we pay taxes to Caesar or not? Isn't it wrong to do so?

**Narrator 4:** They said this to try to get Jesus to tell them to break the law, but instead, he said…

**Jesus:** Why are you trying to trick me? Isn't Caesar's head on the coins? Then give him what is his and give God what is God's.

*Chief priests exit stage right.*

**Narrator 1:** This answer amazed everyone, and they didn't know what to think. No matter how hard the chief priests tried to trick Jesus, it just didn't work. He knew exactly what was going on, and even told his friends that the chief priests would eventually be punished.

**Narrator 2:** Jesus spent a lot of time talking to his disciples and trying to prepare them for what he knew was going to happen. One day, he told them a story about a man who went away from his house and left his servants in charge.

**Jesus:** The man told the servants to stay awake and keep watch. They didn't know when he might be coming back, so they had to be prepared. They didn't want him to find them sleeping. And I'm saying the same to you: keep watch, and do not be found sleeping.

**Narrator 3:** Now the festival of Passover was only two days away and the chief priests, having been unsuccessful so far, were *still* plotting to trick Jesus, arrest him and have him killed.

**Chief priest 3:** (*Offstage*) We can't do anything during the feast. The people may start a riot if we do.

**Narrator 4:** So they kept on secretly plotting. Meanwhile, Jesus and his disciples were eating at the home of a man called Simon when a woman came in, carrying a bottle of very expensive perfume, which she poured over Jesus' head.

*The girl with a bottle of perfume enters stage left. She pours the perfume over Jesus' head.*

**Judas:**     What a waste! We could have sold that perfume for a lot of money and given it to the poor.

**Jesus:**     Leave her alone! What she has done is good. You will always have the poor with you, but you won't always have me. She has poured perfume on my body to prepare it for burial.

**Narrator 5:**     Jesus' words puzzled the disciples, but he knew exactly what he was saying.

*All exit except Judas.*

**Narrator 5:**     It was around this time that Judas Iscariot, one of Jesus' twelve disciples, went to see the chief priests to ask how much they would pay him to betray Jesus.

*Enter chief priests and accusers.*

**Song:** *We want rid of him*

*All exit except Judas, who stays on stage. He mimes to show that he's making a decision.*

 **Props**
- Table
- Tablecloth
- Bread
- Wine (blackcurrant juice) in a clay jug
- Pottery wine goblets (optional)

**Narrator 2:**     The festival of unleavened bread, also known as Passover, was approaching.

*Jesus, Peter and John enter stage left.*

**Jesus:**     Go and prepare the Passover meal for us to eat. In the city you will meet a man carrying a jar of water. Follow him to the house. There you will find an upstairs room ready for you to use. Prepare the meal there.

**Narrator 2:**     So Peter and John went into Jerusalem, found the house and the room, and prepared the Passover meal.

*Peter and John exit and return carrying a tablecloth, bread and wine. They set the table stage left. Jesus and the other disciples enter and sit around the table.*

**Jesus:**     I have been looking forward to eating this meal with you. I won't eat with you again until God's kingdom comes.

**Andrew:**     A new kingdom? We don't know what you mean!

**Narrator 5:**     Jesus took a cup of wine in his hands and said thank you to God for it. He said to his disciples…

**Jesus:**     Take this wine and share it with each other. I will not drink any more wine with you until God's kingdom comes.

**Narrator 4:**     Jesus took some bread in his hands and said thank you to God for it. He broke the bread and handed it to his disciples.

Reproduced with permission from *This Man Called Jesus* published by BRF 2005 (1 84101 434 6) www.barnabasinschools.org.uk

**Jesus:** This is my body, which is given for you. Eat this as a way of remembering me!

**Narrator 4:** The disciples ate the bread and drank the wine, just as Jesus told them to.

**Jesus:** One of you sitting here at this table is going to betray me and hand me over to the chief priests. What a terrible thing that will be!

**Narrator 3:** The disciples started arguing about who would do such a thing.

**Narrator 2:** This led to an argument about which one of them was the greatest.

*The disciples mime arguing with each other. Jesus looks on.*

**Narrator 4:** Jesus taught the disciples that the person who is truly great is not the one who is served, but the one who serves others.

**Jesus:** I have been with you as a servant, even though my Father has given me the right to rule as a king.

**Narrator 4:** Then Jesus took Peter to one side.

**Jesus:** Peter, I pray that your faith will be strong. A time is coming when you will say that you don't know me. I pray that after you have let me down, you will turn back to me and help the others to be faithful.

**Peter:** But I'm not going to let you down! I would die for you if I had to!

**Jesus:** Peter, before the cockerel crows tomorrow morning, you will say three times that you don't know me.

**Narrator 1:** When they had finished their meal, Jesus and his disciples left and went to a garden called Gethsemane, which was on the Mount of Olives. Here Jesus began to pray.

*All exit stage left except Judas.*

**Narrator 1:** But Judas stayed behind. Silently, he crept away unnoticed to continue his plot to betray Jesus.

*Judas creeps off stage right.*

## SCENE 3

### THE GARDEN OF GETHSEMANE

 **Cast**

- ❖ Narrators 1, 2, 3, 4 and 5
- ❖ Jesus
- ❖ Peter
- ❖ John
- ❖ James
- ❖ Other disciples
- ❖ Judas Iscariot
- ❖ Accusers
- ❖ Malchus
- ❖ Caiaphas
- ❖ Servant girls 1, 2 and 3
- ❖ Pilate

 **Props**

- ❖ Swords and clubs

🎵 **Song**

- ❖ Why do we call it Good Friday?

**Narrator 3:** Jesus went with his disciples to a place called Gethsemane. When they got there, he told them, 'Sit here while I go over there and pray.'

*Jesus and the disciples enter stage left. Jesus mimes speaking to the disciples and then, beckoning to Peter, James and John to go with him, he crosses to centre stage. The disciples who are left lie down and go to sleep.*

**Jesus:** I am so sad that I feel as if I am dying. Stay here and keep awake for me.

*Peter, James and John lie down centre stage. Jesus moves apart from them, towards stage right, and kneels down.*

| | |
|---|---|
| **Jesus:** | My Father, if it is possible, don't make me die in this way. But do what you want, and not what I want. |
| **Narrator 4:** | After he had prayed, Jesus came back and found his disciples sleeping. |

*Jesus gets up and crosses back to centre stage.*

| | |
|---|---|
| **Jesus:** | Can't any of you stay awake for me for just one hour? |
| **Peter:** | I am willing, but my body is weak. |
| **Jesus:** | Look, the hour is near. Here comes my betrayer. |

*Judas enters with three or four accusers and Malchus. Some of the accusers are dressed as soldiers.*

| | |
|---|---|
| **Narrator 5:** | Just then Judas appeared, with a large mob armed with swords and clubs. As it was still dark, Judas had arranged to greet Jesus with a light kiss on the cheek, so that the men knew who to arrest. |
| **Judas:** | Hello, teacher. *(He kisses Jesus lightly on the cheek.)* |
| **Jesus:** | My friend, why are you here? |
| **Narrator 3:** | The men grabbed Jesus and arrested him. |
| **Peter:** | No you don't! |

*Peter grabs a sword and lunges at Malchus. The group step back and Malchus clutches his right ear.*

| | |
|---|---|
| **Jesus:** | Put your sword away. |
| **Narrator 1:** | Jesus knew that if he wanted to, he could ask God to send a whole army of angels to rescue him. But that was not the way it was to be. |
| **Narrator 2:** | Instead, Jesus touched Malchus' ear and healed him. |

*Jesus mimes healing Malchus.*

| | |
|---|---|
| **Jesus:** | Why do you come with swords and clubs to arrest me? Day after day |

| | |
|---|---|
| | I sat and taught in the temple, but you didn't arrest me then. |
| **Narrator 4:** | As the mob took Jesus away, all his disciples left him and ran away. |

*The disciples exit stage left. Accusers and Judas exit with Jesus stage right.*

| | |
|---|---|
| **Narrator 3:** | There wasn't time to call for a jury but the Pharisees did have time to pay some people to tell lies about Jesus. |

*Enter Caiaphas, who stands centre stage. Enter accusers and Jesus stage right. Accusers take Jesus to Caiaphas. Peter and the servant girls enter and stand at the back of the stage, half hidden in the wings, watching the proceedings.*

| | |
|---|---|
| **Accuser 1:** | I saw Jesus trying to start a riot. |
| **Caiaphas:** | When? |
| **Accuser 1:** | Er… I… er… I can't remember… |
| **Accuser 2:** | I heard him say he would destroy the temple and rebuild it in three days. |
| **Caiaphas:** | Is this true? |
| **Accuser 2:** | Well, not exactly. He said he could, though! |
| **Caiaphas:** | Jesus? |
| **Jesus:** | Yes? |
| **Caiaphas:** | Is this true? |
| **Narrator 4:** | But Jesus wouldn't answer. |
| **Caiaphas:** | Why don't you say something in your own defence? Can't you hear the charges they are making against you? |
| **Narrator 3:** | Again Jesus wouldn't answer. |
| **Caiaphas:** | With the living God looking on, you must tell the truth. Tell us, are you the Messiah, the Son of God? |
| **Jesus:** | That is what you say! |
| **Caiaphas:** | This man claims to be God! We don't need any more witnesses! You have heard what he said. What do you think? |
| **Accuser 3:** | He is guilty and deserves to die! |
| **Narrator 5:** | Then they spat in his face and hit him with their fists. |

Reproduced with permission from *This Man Called Jesus* published by BRF 2005 (1 84101 434 6) www.barnabasinschools.org.uk

**Narrator 2:** Meanwhile, Peter had followed Jesus to the high priest's house and was sitting out in the courtyard when a servant girl came up to him.

**Servant 1:** Aren't you one of Jesus' friends?

**Peter:** That isn't so! I don't know what you're talking about!

**Narrator 2:** Yet another servant girl said…

**Servant 2:** This man was with Jesus of Nazareth.

**Peter:** No I wasn't! I don't even know the man!

**Servant 3:** We know that you are one of his friends! We can tell because of your accent: you're from Galilee.

**Peter:** I'm telling you the truth! I don't know the man!

**Narrator 4:** At once a cockerel crowed, and Peter remembered that Jesus had said, 'Before the cockerel crows, you will say three times that you don't know me.'

*Jesus turns and looks straight at Peter. Peter hides his face in his hands and runs off stage right.*

**Narrator 4:** Then Peter went out and cried bitterly.

*All exit stage right.*

**Narrator 5:** Early next morning, all the chief priests and the nation's leaders met and decided that Jesus should be put to death. They tied him up and led him away to Pilate the governor.

*Enter Pilate, who stands centre stage. Enter accusers and Jesus stage right. Accusers take Jesus to Pilate.*

**Accuser 3:** This man claims to be the Messiah, God's chosen king.

**Pilate:** Jesus, are you the king of the Jews?

**Jesus:** Those are your words!

**Narrator 4:** And when the chief priests and leaders brought their charges against him, he did not say a thing.

**Pilate:** Don't you hear what crimes they say you have done?

**Narrator 4:** But Jesus did not say anything, and the governor was greatly amazed.

**Narrator 2:** During Passover, the governor always freed a prisoner chosen by the people. At that time, a well-known criminal named Barabbas was in jail. So Pilate asked the crowd…

**Pilate:** Which prisoner do you want me to set free? Do you want Barabbas, or Jesus who is called the Messiah?

**Accusers:** Barabbas! Barabbas!

**Pilate:** What am I to do with this man Jesus?

**Accusers:** Nail him to a cross!

**Pilate** But what crime has he done?

**Accusers:** Nail him to a cross!

**Narrator 1:** There was nothing else to be done. Pilate set Barabbas free. Then he ordered his soldiers to beat Jesus with a whip and nail him to a cross.

*Song: Why do we call it Good Friday?*

*All exit stage right.*

❖

**SCENE 4**

**THE CRUCIFIXION**

 **Cast**

❖ Narrators 1, 2, 3, 4 and 5
❖ Barabbas

 **Props**

❖ A low stool for Barabbas to sit on
❖ Projection screen (optional)
❖ Video player, slide projector or data projector and laptop with PowerPoint for a static display or montage (all optional)

 **Song**

❖ Barabbas' song

**Narrator 1:** The soldiers nailed Jesus to a cross and sat down to guard him. At midday the sky turned dark and stayed that way until three o'clock. Then about that time Jesus shouted out, 'My God, my God, why have you deserted me?'

**Narrator 2:** Some people standing nearby heard Jesus cry out. One of them ran and grabbed a sponge. He soaked it in wine, then put it on a stick and held it up to Jesus.

**Narrator 1:** Once again Jesus cried out.

**Narrator 3:** And then he died.

**Narrator 4:** At once the curtain in the temple was torn in two from top to bottom.

**Narrator 5:** The earth shook, and rocks split apart. The officer and the soldiers guarding Jesus felt the earthquake and were very frightened. They said…

**All Narrators:** This man called Jesus really was God's Son!

*Barabbas enters and sits centre stage with his head in his hands.*

**Narrator 1:** Meanwhile, Barabbas was back in his cell, waiting to be set free the next day. He had a lot to think about. He had thought he was going to be killed, but this man Jesus was being beaten and nailed to a cross in his stead. He knew Jesus hadn't done anything wrong. Barabbas knew all the crooks and thieves in the city of Jerusalem— and Jesus wasn't one of them. Who was Jesus, and why was he being punished for all the wrong things that Barabbas had done? What was he going to do with his life, now that he had a second chance?

*Narrators 2, 3, 4 and 5 take it in turn to read out the creative writing work on Barabbas previously written by the children. As the pieces*

*are being read, project images of the cross on to the screen at the back of the stage (see page 31 for suggestions as to how to create a video, slide show or PowerPoint montage).*

**Song:** *Barabbas' song*

*The song can be sung as a solo by Barabbas, or by another child chosen to perform the solo. If the latter, Barabbas retains his position centre stage while the song is being sung.*

---

**SCENE 5**

**THE RESURRECTION**

 **Cast**

❖ Narrators 1, 2, 3, 4 and 5
❖ Mary
❖ Salome
❖ Peter
❖ James
❖ John
❖ Thomas
❖ Disciples (except Judas)
❖ Jesus

 **Songs**

❖ Clap your hands, shout hallelujah
❖ Jesus is living

---

**Narrator 3:** That evening, a rich man called Joseph who lived in the town of Arimathea went and asked for Jesus' body. He wrapped Jesus' body in a clean linen cloth and laid him in a tomb that had been cut from solid rock. He rolled a big stone against the entrance and went away.

**Narrator 4:** The women who had come with Jesus from Galilee followed Joseph and watched how Jesus' body was placed in the tomb.

Reproduced with permission from *This Man Called Jesus* published by BRF 2005 (1 84101 434 6) www.barnabasinschools.org.uk

**Narrator 5:** Very early on Sunday morning, the women went to the tomb, carrying some spices they had prepared. When they found the stone rolled away from the entrance, they went in. But they did not find the body of Jesus.

**Narrator 2:** Quickly they ran back to the house in Jerusalem where the disciples were hiding behind locked doors, for fear that the soldiers would try to arrest them too.

*The disciples enter stage left. They sit together on the floor, quietly talking together and praying. Mary and Salome enter stage right. They stop centre stage and pretend to bang on the door.*

**Mary:** Let us in! Let us in!
**Salome:** Quickly! Let us in!
**Peter:** Who is it?
**Mary:** It's us.
**Salome:** Mary and Salome.
**James:** Let them in.
**Thomas:** What's all the noise?
**John:** What's happened?
**Mary:** We went to the tomb where Jesus is buried.
**Salome:** Someone had moved the huge stone.
**Mary:** And Jesus isn't there.
**Salome:** But there were two men there.
**Mary:** We were terrified!
**Salome:** They told us not to be afraid.
**Mary:** One of them told us that Jesus has risen from the dead.
**Thomas:** I've never heard such nonsense!

*Thomas exits stage left.*

**Narrator 5:** But Peter wanted to see for himself, so he ran to the tomb. When he stooped down and looked in, he saw only the burial clothes. Then he returned, wondering what had happened.

*Peter exits stage right. After a short while he returns stage right. He is walking slowly and looking stunned.*

**Peter:** The women are right. He's not there.

*Peter sits back down with the rest of the group. They look frightened and confused.*

**Narrator 2:** The disciples still didn't know what this all meant. That evening they locked themselves in the upstairs room, frightened and confused.

*Jesus enters stage right.*

**Jesus:** Peace be with you.
**John:** Jesus!
**Jesus:** I am sending you, just as the Father sent me.
**Andrew:** It's really you!
**James:** Everything you said has come true!

*Song: Clap your hands, shout hallelujah*

*During the singing of the song, Jesus stands centre back of the stage, looking on.*

*Enter Thomas stage left. He rejoins the group.*

**Narrator 2:** Thomas wasn't with the others when Jesus appeared to them, and when they told him that they had seen Jesus, he wouldn't believe them. A week later, when Thomas was with the disciples in the upstairs room, Jesus came in while the door was still locked.

*Jesus steps forward and addresses the group.*

**Jesus:** Peace be with you. Thomas, look at my hands! Put your finger in my side. Have faith and stop doubting!
**Thomas:** You are my Lord and my God!
**Jesus:** Do you have faith because you have seen me, Thomas? The people who

Reproduced with permission from *This Man Called Jesus* published by BRF 2005 (1 84101 434 6) www.barnabasinschools.org.uk

have faith in me without seeing me are the ones who are really blessed!

*All exit stage left.*

**Narrator 1:** After that, Jesus appeared many times to his disciples. One day, the disciples decided to go fishing. They went out in their boat, but didn't catch a thing all night.

*The disciples enter stage left. They take up positions centre stage as if they are in a boat, casting their net over the side.*

**Narrator 2:** Early the next morning, Jesus stood on the shore. He called to the disciples.

*Jesus enters stage left and stands near the front of the stage.*

**Jesus:** Cast your net on the other side!
**Narrator 3:** They did, and the net was so full of fish that they could not drag it up into the boat.

*The disciples mime trying to drag a huge catch of fish into the boat.*

**Narrator 4:** Peter looked to the shore and realized…
**Peter:** It's Jesus!

*Peter mimes jumping out of the boat and wading to shore. He and Jesus sit down together. The rest of the disciples freeze their poses.*

**Jesus:** Peter?
**Peter:** Jesus, I'm so sorry. I didn't mean to… I mean, I tried…
**Jesus:** Peter…
**Peter:** Yes, Lord?
**Jesus:** It's OK.
**Peter:** But I let you down… I let you die!
**Jesus:** Peter…
**Peter:** Yes, Lord?

**Jesus:** That's why I had to die.

*The other disciples mime dragging the boat to shore. They join Peter and Jesus and sit in a group, miming eating and chatting.*

**Narrator 5:** The day came for Jesus to leave his friends and return once more to his Father in heaven.

*Jesus stands up, while the disciples continue to sit on the stage at his feet.*

**Jesus:** I have been given all authority in heaven and on earth! Go to the people of all nations and make them my disciples. Baptize them in the name of the Father, the Son and the Holy Spirit, and teach them to do everything I have told you. I will be with you always, even until the end of the world.

*Jesus exits stage left.*

**Song:** *Jesus is living*

*The rest of the cast join the disciples on stage during the song, waving palm branches as they sing.*

THE END

# Song sheets

# Jesus is coming

Jesus is coming, Jesus is coming,
Jesus is coming to Jerusalem.

Hosanna in the highest,
Hosanna in the highest,
Hosanna to the son of David.

Blessed is he, blessed is he,
Blessed is he, blessed is he,
Blessed is he who comes in the name of the Lord.

# We want rid of him

We want rid of him,
He gives us so much trouble.
We want rid of him,
Quickly, at the double.
If he stays here
We'll be out on our ear,
Let's kill this man called Jesus.

See Judas there,
He looks a little shifty.
A friend of Jesus Christ,
But if we give him money
He may think twice.
At a very good price
He'll help get rid of Jesus.

So Judas, will you
Help get rid of Jesus?
We'll pay you well
If you hand him over to us.
You say you will?
Well, then, give us the bill,
Let's go and find this Jesus.

Reproduced with permission from *This Man Called Jesus* published by BRF 2005 (1 84101 434 6) **www.barnabasinschools.org.uk**

# Why do we call it Good Friday?

Why do we call it Good Friday?
A day when we think
Of your death!
You died on the cross
Like a criminal,
But we remember it today.

Jesus, your death
Wasn't the end,
In fact it was just the beginning.
When you died on the cross
You gave hope to the world.
You dealt with the
Wrongs we've all done.

Why do we call it Good Friday?
Because you took all the blame.
The wrongs we have done
Needed punishing,
But you did that by taking our place.

# Barabbas' song

I stand here amazed
At what you've done for me,
Taking my place upon the cross
So that I could be set free.
I don't deserve to be saved,
I've done wrong in many ways,
But still you quietly took the blame,
And so I give you praise.

## Chorus
**Jesus, you saved me from the cross**
**I thank you and praise God on high.**
**For giving me another chance**
**I worship and thank you today.**

How can I ever repay
The gift you've given today?
Why should you show me this love,
Giving your life in this way?
I'm more grateful than I'll ever know,
So changing my life will show,
In turning from sin and changing within,
My praise is living for you.

## Chorus...

# Clap your hands, shout hallelujah

**Chorus**
**Clap your hands, shout hallelujah,**
**For Jesus has risen today. (x 2)**

The tomb where he lay is empty.
His body is really not there.
The stone's rolled away,
The guards are amazed,
Jesus is alive!

## Chorus...

Jesus had said what would happen:
When three days had passed,
He would rise!
The third day has come,
A new age has dawned,
Jesus is alive!

## Chorus...

Through rising from death,
He has shown us
That he is the true Son of God.
Friendship with him
For all who believe,
Jesus is alive!

## Chorus...

Reproduced with permission from *This Man Called Jesus* published by BRF 2005 (1 84101 434 6) **www.barnabasinschools.org.uk**

# Jesus is living

Jesus is living, Jesus is living,
Jesus is living and will come again.

Hosanna in the highest,
Hosanna in the highest,
Hosanna to the son of David.

Blessed is he, blessed is he,
Blessed is he, blessed is he,
Blessed is he who comes in the name of the Lord.

# Sheet music
# for the songs

# Jesus is coming

Eleanor Jeans

This song can be sung as a round. Divide the singers into three equal groups. Group 1 begins at ①. Group 2 begins when Group 1 reaches ② and Group 3 begins when Group 1 reaches ③.

Percussion idea: shakers could play repeated quavers all the way through the song.

# We want rid of him

♩ = 120-132

Eleanor Jeans

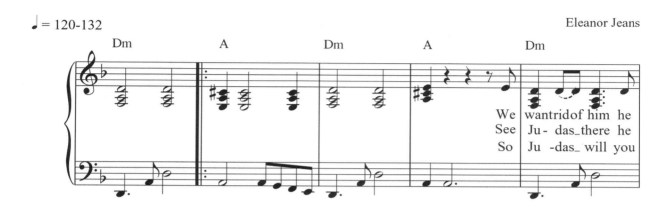

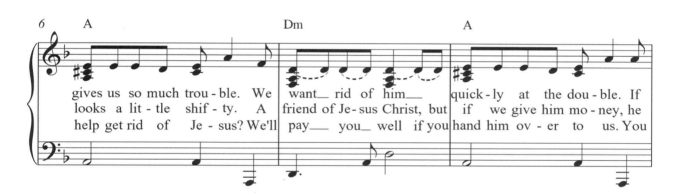

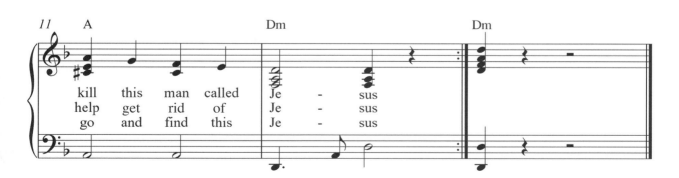

# Why do we call it Good Friday?

Eleanor Jeans

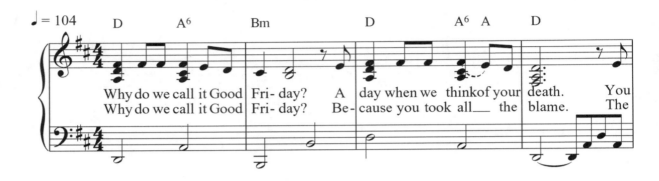

Why do we call it Good Fri- day? A day when we think of your death. You
Why do we call it Good Fri- day? Be- cause you took all the blame. The

died on the cross like a cri - mi - nal but we re - mem - ber it to - day
wrongs we have done need - ed pun - ish - ing but you did that by tak - ing our place

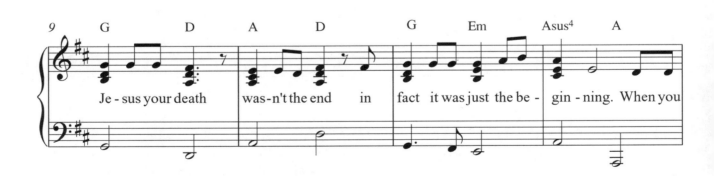

Je - sus your death was-n't the end in fact it was just the be - gin - ning. When you

died   on   the   cross   you   gave   hope   to   the   world,   you

**D.C. al Fine**

dealt   with   the wrongs we've   all   done_____

# Barabbas' song

Eleanor Jeans

# Clap your hands, shout hallelujah

Eleanor Jeans

# Jesus is living

Eleanor Jeans

This song can be sung as a round. Divide the singers into three equal groups. Group 1 begins at ①. Group 2 begins when Group 1 reaches ② and Group 3 begins when Group 1 reaches ③.

Percussion idea: shakers could play repeated quavers all the way through the song.

# Bibliography

Below is a list of resources that you may find helpful. They range from websites with useful information to extra songs that you may wish to include in the performance or listen to as part of a music lesson.

## ENGLISH

### Bibles

New Century Version: International Children's Bible, published by Authentic Bibles

*The Lion Storyteller Bible*, published by Lion Hudson

THE MESSAGE, published by NavPress

Good News Bible, published by The Bible Societies/ HarperCollins

Contemporary English Version, published by Bible Society/HarperCollins

Contemporary English Version Popular Schools, published by Bible Society

Contemporary English Version Youth Bible, published by Bible Society/HarperCollins

New International Version, published by Hodder and Stoughton

### Other books

*Animal Tales*, Butterworth and Inkpen, published by Zondervan

## MUSIC

### Recorded music

Handel's *Messiah*

Bach's *St Matthew Passion* or *St John Passion*

*Godspell*

Stainer's *Crucifixion*

### Other songs to listen to or sing

Matt Redman: Jesus Christ, I think upon your sacrifice

Martyn Layzell: You chose the cross

Graham Kendrick: From heaven you came

Melody Green: There is a redeemer

Isaac Watts: When I survey the wondrous cross

Stuart Townend: How deep the Father's love for us

Rick Founds: Lord I lift your name on high

Gerald Coates, Noel and Tricia Richards: He has risen

Arr. Townend: Were you there?

Graham Kendrick: No scenes of stately majesty

The sheet music for all of the above songs can be found in the *Songs of Fellowship* books published by Kingsway (www.kingsway.co.uk)

For more general songs (some reflecting the Easter message), try Vineyard Music's *Great Big God* CDs (www.vineyardmusic.co.uk)

For recordings of some of the above songs, try 'Wellspring' (www.wellspring.org.uk)

Visit www.musicforyouth.org for other ideas about singing.

### Songs to warm up to

Frère Jacques

London's Burning

Cockles and Mussels

Appleby and Fowler, *Sing Together*, published by Oxford University Press, has some simple folk songs that are great.

## RE

### Videos

*The Miracle Maker* (Icon Home Entertainment)

*Prince of Egypt* (Dreamworks)

*Story Keepers* (www.storykeepers.com)

*The Easter Carol* (Veggie Tales)

*Jesus of Nazareth* (Carlton, 1977)

### Passover

*Why on This Night?: A Passover Haggadah for Family Celebration*, Rahel Musleah, published by Simon Pulse.

See www.faithcentral.net.nz/inclass/chapel/passover.htm for an online Passover resource.

## Communion

*Welcome to the Lord's Table* by Margaret Withers, published by BRF

*Come and Join the Celebration* by Muir and Pedley, published by Church House Publishing

## Other books

*Theme Games* Volume 1, Lesley Pinchbeck, published by Scripture Union

## ORGANIZATIONS

'Walk thru the Bible': www.bible.org.uk produce sessions called 'Bible Explorer' for schools.

## WEBSITES

### Art and design

Culham College runs a website full of links to classic works of art depicting the Easter story: www.refuel.org.uk/curric/festivals/easter

### ICT

www.teachingideas.co.uk/ict/contents.htm is a website with lots of ICT links.

Try the image search on www.google.co.uk